LIFE-CHANGING PRAYERS

Discover the Power of Prayer

Contributing writers: Randy Petersen, Marie D. Jones, Wallis C. Metts, Gary Wilde

Acknowledgments:
Unless otherwise noted, Scripture quotations are taken from the *New Revised Standard Version* of the Bible. Copyright © 1989 by the Division of Christian Education of the National Council of the Churches of Christ in the USA. Used by permission. All rights reserved.

Scripture quotation marked (NKJV) is taken from the *New King James Version*. Copyright © 1979, 1980, 1982 by Thomas Nelson, Inc. Used by permission. All rights reserved.

Scripture quotations marked (NLT) are taken from *The Holy Bible*, New Living Translation, copyright © 1996. Used by permission of Tyndale House Publishers, Inc. All rights reserved.

Louis Weber, CEO
Publications International, Ltd.
7373 North Cicero Avenue
Lincolnwood, Illinois 60712

Manufactured in U.S.A.

8 7 6 5 4 3 2 1

ISBN: 0-7853-8251-8

CONTENTS

PRAYER ENRICHES OUR LIVES

PRAYER IS REALLY just talking to God—sharing our hopes, our dreams, our fears, and our heartaches with the only One who understands us completely. God yearns to be close to us, to be a part of our lives. God wants us to turn to him whenever we feel weak, scared, or alone and need someone who can help us.

Does prayer have to use special, fancy language? No. Does it have to occur in a traditional religious setting? No, most of the prayers in this book didn't. Does it have to be an urgent request? No, many prayers simply praise our great and wonderful God.

There are many different types of prayers: prayers for help and growth, prayers of repentance, prayers of praise, even prayers of questioning.

The beautiful prayers in this book were written by various spiritual leaders—from the apostle Paul and St. Augustine to Amy Carmichael and Reinhold Niebuhr—during their own personal moments of need or thanksgiving.

You may wish to spend a few relaxing moments with this book on a hectic day, reading through a prayer or two alone, during a time of quiet. At other times you might need several soothing prayers to ease your weary, troubled mind.

In either case, remember that prayer is both an *action* and an *attitude.*

We pray whenever we create space in our day to share with God. We pray with our words, but we can also pray without words. For God not only knows our minds, but he sees the depths of our hearts. He sees us as we truly are, so he always knows what we need.

This isn't just a book you read; it's a book you *use.* Use it to jump-start a stalled relationship with God. Use it to break new ground in your communication with God. Use it to come even closer to the Lord you love.

CHAPTER ONE

LEARNING
to
PRAY

JESUS LOVES ME
Anna B. Warner

Jesus loves me! This I know,
for the Bible tells me so.
Little ones to him belong;
they are weak, but he is strong.
Yes, Jesus loves me! Yes, Jesus loves me!
Yes, Jesus loves me! The Bible tells me so.

CHILDLIKE FAITH

WHEN ANNA B. WARNER wrote this hymn in 1860, it was part of a poem that appeared with a novel co-written with Anna's sister, Susan. But it wasn't long before this simple declaration of Jesus' love for his children became a universally loved hymn. All across the globe, it is sung by children and adults in dozens of languages.

For many of us, this hymn was the first one we learned to speak or sing in church or Sunday school. It introduced us to God's promise of love, as told in the Bible through Jesus. With a child's innocence, the words speak to us of a truth that cannot be disputed: Once we turn to Jesus, we will forever be loved and cared for by him. After all, the Bible tells us so. Especially powerful is the line "they are weak, but he is strong," for this means that we have a champion in heaven who cares if we are weak or scared. Jesus told us we must become like children if we are to enter the kingdom of God, and this simple hymn reminds us all—no matter our age—of this wonderful truth.

THE MIND OF A CHILD
Matthew 11:25–26

At that time Jesus said, "I thank you, Father, Lord of heaven and earth, because you have hidden these things from the wise and the intelligent and have revealed them to infants; yes, Father, for such was your gracious will."

THE WISDOM OF INNOCENCE

IN THIS PRAYER, Jesus emphasizes that anyone can grasp the truths conveyed in the gospel message. You don't have to be especially intelligent or educated; in fact, you need only have an open mind like a child's.

There is nothing wrong with pursuing worldly knowledge, but when it comes to connecting with God, children know something most adults have forgotten: The mind has little to do with it. Knowing and loving God is in the realm of the heart in its most childlike state of innocence and trust.

SIMPLE DELIVERANCE
Psalm 116:1–7

I love the Lord, because he has heard my voice and my supplications. Because he inclined his ear to me, therefore I will call on him as long as I live. The snares of death encompassed me; the pangs of Sheol laid hold on me; I suffered distress and anguish. Then I called on the name of the Lord: "O Lord, I pray, save my life!"

Gracious is the Lord, and righteous; our God is merciful. The Lord protects the simple; when I was brought low, he saved me. Return, O my soul, to your rest, for the Lord has dealt bountifully with you.

CALL OUT IN FAITH

IN THIS PRAYER, David recalled how the Lord had answered his previous prayer. In fact, because God had heard and answered his prayers in the past, David was determined to call on God as long as he lived.

David had prayed during the darkest moments of his life—when King Saul hunted him and while he hid in the caves of Judea. David lived like a fugitive, forced at times to seek shelter with the traditional enemies of his people.

Nevertheless, David was convinced that a gracious and merciful God had saved him whenever he asked for deliverance. Ultimately, David received more than he asked for: a throne of his own and the promise of a bright future.

What changed David's life? Part of the answer is in this prayer. David says the Lord protects the simple, and his own prayer had been basic: He called out for God to save him, and God did.

David prayed with the faith of a child; he then discovered that the Lord protects the simple and answers their prayers.

Quiet My Heart
16th-century Frankfurt prayer

Lord, teach me to silence my own heart that I may listen to the gentle movement of the Holy Spirit within me and sense the depths which are of God.

A DIVINE VOICE

THIS BEAUTIFUL 16TH-CENTURY PRAYER compels us to follow the voice of the Lord for the guidance we need. Often we let our emotions drown out his words to us. When we follow our feelings without consulting God, we end up overreacting or acting impulsively.

If we could learn to become still and pray while it is quiet, we might just hear something stirring deep within our hearts—a divine voice speaking to us.

GOD, GRANT ME SERENITY
Reinhold Niebuhr

God grant me the serenity to accept the things I cannot change, the courage to change the things I can, and the wisdom to know the difference.

PEACE OF MIND

REINHOLD NIEBUHR, A 20th-century American theologian, prayed this prayer, which is now quoted in one form or another throughout the world. This request for God's blessings has been a life-changing inspiration to millions of believers.

How we need serenity, courage, and wisdom in our lives! Our days will be transformed when we slow down and develop these godly virtues. If we can learn how and when to put them to good use, nothing will disturb our peace.

Day by Day
Richard of Chichester

May I know You more clearly,
Love You more dearly,
And follow You more nearly,
Day by day.

Walk Closely With God

RICHARD OF CHICHESTER studied at Oxford and Paris before becoming chancellor of Oxford University in 1235. Then, in 1244, he began a new era of his life, becoming the Bishop of Chichester. There he decided on a lifelong goal of elevating the level of spirituality among the people in his area.

Richard's poetic prayer gives evidence of his heartfelt desire to walk closely with God. These words were put to song some years ago, and they certainly retain their life-changing power to this day. If we were to offer the sentiments of this simple prayer each morning, desiring to follow his will, we would surely grow in our sense of God's abiding nearness.

MULLER'S LIFE OF PRAYER
George Muller

*Dear Father, we thank thee
for what thou art going to give us to eat.*

PRAYING FOR THE NEEDS OF OTHERS

AT FIRST GLANCE, this prayer may seem rather unusual. Although George Muller thanked God for his provision, he had no food to feed the children in his orphanage in Bristol, England. Within minutes, however, a baker knocked on the door and brought fresh bread he had made the night before when he couldn't sleep. Then the driver of a milk wagon stopped at the orphanage. His wagon had broken down, and he wondered if Muller knew anyone who could use the milk, since otherwise it would surely spoil while he tried to repair the wagon.

This prayer was characteristic of "Daddy Muller," a man who became a father to the fatherless, caring for more than 10,000 children. In 1830, as a young pastor, he vowed to trust God completely to supply his needs.

Over the next 68 years, he started three orphanages and raised more than seven million dollars. His own salary was about $12,000 a year, most of which he gave away. Muller read the Bible through more than 200 times, and he prayed almost constantly.

Muller was a compassionate man with an unusual gift for prayer. The key to his prayer was specificity—praying for the needs of others.

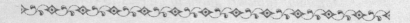

BE ALERT AND PRAY
Luke 22:39–46 NLT

Then, accompanied by his disciples, Jesus left the upstairs room and went as usual to the Mount of Olives. There he told them, "Pray that you will not be overcome by temptation." He walked away, about a stone's throw, and knelt down and prayed, "Father, if you are willing, please take

this cup of suffering away from me. Yet I want your will,
not mine."

Then an angel from heaven appeared and strengthened him.
He prayed more fervently, and he was in such agony of
spirit that his sweat fell to the ground like great drops
of blood.

At last he stood up again and returned to the disciples,
only to find them asleep, exhausted from grief. "Why are
you sleeping?" he asked. "Get up and pray. Otherwise
temptation will overpower you."

PRAY ALWAYS

MOST OF US would like to pray as Jesus did—with such passion that the ground would be wet with our blood-like sweat. We would also like to pray for the same thing: that the Father's will would be done. The truth is, in learning how to pray, we have to start with the same problem the disciples had: how to stay awake. Why is it that when we should be praying, we are often sleeping? The eyes close, the head nods, and we find ourselves falling asleep in the comfort of our bed. The disciples had been through a hard week. They had good intentions, but when they reclined on the grass in the Garden of Gethsemane, they went right to sleep. So the second time Jesus asked them to pray, he told them to "get up," which isn't a bad idea.

The real reason the disciples couldn't stay awake, however, was because they didn't know what was going to happen. If they had known a band of soldiers was coming to take Jesus prisoner, they would have been wide awake, calling on God for help.

We don't know what's going to happen, either. That's a good reason for us to be diligent. Jesus said, "Get up and pray. Otherwise temptation will overpower you." It is important to keep this advice in mind at all times—to be alert and pray.

THE SIGN OF THE CROSS

In the name of the Father,
and of the Son,
and of the Holy Spirit, amen.

INVITING GOD INTO OUR LIVES

THE WORDS TO "The Sign of the Cross" are second nature to many Christians throughout the world. At an early age, children learn to move their right hand to their forehead as they say, "In the name of the Father," then move their right hand to their chest as they say "and the Son," and then touch their right hand to their left shoulder and across to their right shoulder as they say, "and of the Holy Spirit," and then clasp their hands together as they say, "amen."

This gesture, acted out at the beginning and ending of prayers, symbolizes many things to Christians. It represents belief in Christ, and it also represents the cross at Calvary, where Jesus died to save us. "The Sign of the Cross" and its accompanying prayer are reverent displays of faith and trust in the Lord. They are our shield against anything that would do us harm.

When we make "The Sign of the Cross," we invite God into our lives. Whether we are praying in times of fear and temptation or as a demonstration of belief, "The Sign of the Cross" brings us closer to God's comfort, love, and strength.

BOTH BIG AND SMALL
Mother Teresa

Here I am, Lord, body, heart and soul.
Grant that with your love,
I may be big enough to reach the world,
And small enough to be at one with you.

A Vibrant Spiritual Life

MANY OF US, when we approach the spiritual life, see only two options: We either give ourselves to social service to help those in need, or we move inward in a life-long pursuit of fellowship with God.

Mother Teresa was able to combine both of these callings of the Spirit. This prayer declares her desire to be both big and small: to be big in acts of human kindness but small enough to know God as fully as possible.

Both approaches to religion can change our lives. Let us attempt them, and let us take Mother Teresa's example to heart. She was best known for her selfless acts of compassion, yet she had the time and energy to maintain a vibrant spiritual life, writing numerous prayers and devotions for her fellow workers.

Perhaps Mother Teresa's greatest lesson to us is this: It is always best to keep big and small together. That way, we can give our best to both the Creator and humanity.

CHAPTER TWO

THREE ESSENTIAL PRAYERS

THE POWERFUL
PRAYER OF JABEZ
1 Chronicles 4:10
❧❧❧

Oh that you would bless me indeed and enlarge my border,
and that your hand might be with me, and that you would
keep me from harm that it may not pain me!

THE UNCOVERING OF JABEZ

EVERYTHING WE KNOW about Jabez comes from two verses in 1 Chronicles. This chronicle of Israel's history begins with several chapters of names—starting with Adam and continuing through all the kings of Judah. This is important biographical data, but it is not very entertaining.

In chapter 4 the names stop, and we are introduced to an interesting man: "Jabez was honored more than his brothers." We aren't told why he was honored, but throughout this book the chronicler draws a connection between success and relationship with God. If Jabez received great honor, it's likely he was on good terms with his Creator.

The name Jabez is a pun on the word *pain*. We're told that his mother named him. Given the pain of childbirth, it's surprising that there weren't more children named Jabez.

It's curious that he was named by his mother; naming was often the father's right. In fact, there's no mention of his father, which causes us to wonder if the father had died (providing another reason for the name "Pain").

This is speculation, of course, since the Bible tells us so little about Jabez. But we do have a parallel story in Genesis: Jacob's beloved wife Rachel died while bearing Benjamin, so Benjamin, along with Joseph, Rachel's other son, was honored more than his brothers. Joseph and Benjamin were living reminders of a beloved deceased spouse. Perhaps Jabez was honored for the same reason.

UNDERSTANDING THE PRAYER

AFTER WE MEET Jabez and learn the circumstances of his birth, we hear his prayer. Jabez prays for four basic things: blessing, enlarged borders, God's helping hand, and protection.

First, he asks God to bless him. This word is used often in the Old Testament, and God is usually the subject of the verse. The first chapter of the Bible tells us that God blessed the first humans, telling them to "be fruitful and multiply" (Genesis 1:28). Later, God blessed Noah and Abraham, promising to "bless those who bless you" (Genesis 12:3).

What is blessing? To bless is to make good things happen for someone or to wish for or speak those good things. When

God blesses, the wishing, speaking, and making are all wrapped up together. Jabez wanted a life pleasing to God.

Next, Jabez asks God to enlarge his border. In an agrarian society like ancient Israel, more land meant more wealth, but also more responsibility. It would take effort to farm a large plot, but Jabez was determined to meet the challenge.

Don't pray this prayer looking to get rich, though—that's not what Jabez's prayer was about. Pray for enlarged opportunities to serve the Lord. Ask for a new awareness of your gifts and new chances to use them. Ask for sensitivity to the needs of those around you.

Third, Jabez prays that God's hand might be with him. The hand of God is a source of strength. Think of an actual hand guiding your every step. That's what God's hand does throughout Scripture. Jabez knew he needed that support.

This is a prayer guaranteed to be answered affirmatively. God has promised to be with us: "I will never leave you or forsake you" (Hebrews 13:5). We go through times when we are less aware of his presence, but he's always there for us.

Finally, Jabez asks for protection from harm and pain. It is interesting that in this last request, Jabez uses the Hebrew word his mother chose as his name. It is also interesting that he uses two words *(harm* and *pain)* instead of choosing just one. This could be interpreted many different ways. It's possible that he doesn't want to be hurt or to cause hurt, either. Or he might be talking about short-term pain and long-term damage. Or physical injury and spiritual injury. Or maybe he just uses two words to mean the same thing. In any case, he wants God's protective shield.

God has never promised us a life free from pain. In fact, Jesus said, "In the world you face persecution" (John 16:33). But we certainly can ask for God's protection, especially if that means we'll be able to "enlarge our borders"—that is, expand our ministry.

For Jabez, enlarging his borders might have meant doing battle. In that case, he was asking for God's blessing on the endeavor, God's empowering hand, and safety in the struggle. If we apply that to our efforts to live more fully for Christ, it might mean stepping outside our comfort zone and becoming more vulnerable to all sorts of injuries—physical, spiritual, emotional, etc. We should not hesitate to ask God to protect us from harm and pain.

THE SHEPHERD PSALM
Psalm 23

The Lord is my shepherd, I shall not want.
He makes me lie down in green pastures;

he leads me beside still waters,
he restores my soul.
He leads me in right paths for his name's sake.
Even though I walk through the darkest valley,
I fear no evil;
for you are with me;
your rod and your staff—they comfort me.
You prepare a table before me in the presence
of my enemies;
you anoint my head with oil;
my cup overflows.
Surely goodness and mercy shall follow me
all the days of my life,
and I shall dwell in the house of the Lord
my whole life long.

DELIGHTING IN GOD'S PROTECTION

THE BIBLE HAS more than 500 references to sheep or shepherds. In ancient Israel, herding was a common trade. Of course, the biblical writers often used it as a metaphor for our relationship with God. Nowadays, we might say the Lord is my firefighter or the Lord is my construction worker, and we'd develop whole analogies based on these trades. But most people would agree that there's a certain nostalgic beauty in the ancient image of the shepherd. So let's go back to a different time and enter David's world of sheep and shepherds.

If we were to pray Psalm 23 truthfully, we might have to say, "When the Lord is my shepherd, I do not want." In our world, there are many sheep in shepherd's clothing, and they bombard us with all-too-perfect promises of the greenest pastures and the quietest waters. Yet, when we follow them, we soon discover it's all a mirage. We're left standing in a desert, weary from hunger and thirst. Who are we following, and why?

Look around you and you'll see a herd of false shepherds calling for your attention. What would happen if you completed the following sentences honestly?

"When I am my shepherd..."
"When my friends are my shepherd..."
"When money is my shepherd..."

It's obvious that none of these can lead to the satisfaction found in the green pastures God has set aside for us. They can't satisfy our ultimate hunger or quench the thirst of our souls. Only when the Lord is our shepherd do we feel satisfied with who we are and what we have.

"Life is a journey," proclaims one recent TV commercial. The psalmist would agree. We are being led to green pastures, beside still waters, and through the darkest valley. We might try this journey on our own, afraid to ask directions, but ultimately we'll get lost and end up in a ditch somewhere. Elsewhere, the Bible says, "All we like sheep have gone astray; we have all turned to our own way"

(Isaiah 53:6). But Jesus tells of a shepherd who leaves the flock safe in its fold to hunt for one stray lamb. The shepherd then rejoices when he finds the lamb that had been lost. Jesus explains that the stray lamb that is found is like the sinner who repents, causing great joy in heaven (Luke 15:3–7). Psalm 23 helps us to hear the shepherd's voice and return to him.

Dark valleys can confuse us. We go through periods of suffering and doubt when we're not sure where our shepherd is or whether he still cares about us. And we don't know what dangers are lurking in the shadows. But this psalm communicates a faith that works even in the dark: If our shepherd has been leading us through the idyllic pastures without fail, why would he abandon us in the danger zones? He wouldn't, of course! He is with us, so what do we have to fear?

David, the shepherd-king credited with writing this psalm, once boasted about killing a lion and a bear that were threatening his sheep. This psalm certainly doesn't deny the existence of dangerous forces; it just explains that we have a shepherd who will wrestle them into submission. It's a dangerous world, and some valleys are darker than others, but the Lord will protect us. Note also that we walk through the darkest valley—but with the faith that God will lead us out of it. The outcome of trying times may not be what we expect, but God promises to be with us from start to finish.

In the second part of this psalm, it's time to celebrate. The Lord leads us to safety and then throws a banquet for us. Now we see the Lord in a new light. As our shepherd, he guided us through the ups and downs of life. He has shown himself to be strong, wise, and protective. But now at the banquet he is joyful and generous. Amazingly, he is serving us. Jesus once said that he did not come "to be served, but to serve" (Mark 10:45). That's what we see here.

This psalm begins with a picture of the Lord leading us. It ends with his great love following us. God's goodness and mercy attend us wherever we go. They may not always be evident, but they are always there. When we allow God to be our Shepherd, we know we have nothing to fear.

THE LORD'S PRAYER
Matthew 6:9–13

Our Father in heaven,
hallowed be your name.
Your kingdom come.
Your will be done,
on earth as it is in heaven.
Give us this day our daily bread.
And forgive us our debts,

as we also have forgiven our debtors.
And do not bring us to the time of trial,
but rescue us from the evil one.

COMMON GROUND

THERE'S SOMETHING IRONIC about reciting the Lord's Prayer. Most Christians learn it early in life or soon after they commit to Christ. Many churches recite it each week. Countless believers turn to it in times of need. Eventually they can speak the words from memory, without even thinking about them.

Without even thinking about them! There's the irony. Just a few moments before he gave his followers this prayer, Jesus cautioned them to avoid the errors of "the Gentiles" who "heap up empty phrases" because "they think that they will be heard because of their many words" (Matthew 6:7). All too often we have turned the Lord's Prayer into exactly that: empty phrases (the King James Version uses the term "vain repetitions"). We begin to treat this prayer like magic words that will get us what we want. That's certainly not what Jesus intended.

Does that mean we should never recite the Lord's Prayer? Not at all. It provides an ideal meeting ground for public prayer. When any group of believers prays together, they need a common text. Ideally, each person would silently fill in the personal details of the "daily bread" they need or the trial they face. And there are also moments when we as individuals don't know what to pray. We feel distant from God or unsure of what to say. In such times, you can't go wrong with the Lord's own prayer. These words can prime the pump of faith and get you back on speaking terms with your Father in heaven.

FROM RELATIONSHIP TO RESCUE

JESUS' PRAYER begins with relationship. Other Jewish prayers of the time hailed God as the King of the Universe, the Creator of All, and that's very appropriate. Yes, he is that, but the revolutionary teaching of Jesus was that God loves every single one of us, just as a parent loves each of his own children.

The world is full of people who do not completely understand the words they grew up praying. One example of this is *hallowed,* and it simply means holy. As we read the Old Testament, we see people and things becoming "holy" as they connect with God. Holiness seems to be godliness, and it goes without saying that God is godly. But we get a clue from the English language: Holy is related to the word *whole.* When we come in contact with God, he makes us whole, complete. He is the essence of wholeness, and we find our wholeness in him. So don't get scared away by the idea of God being "hallowed" or holy. It just means that he has what you're lacking.

Jesus spent a lot of time preaching about God's kingdom. He told stories about it using comparisons people could relate to. Jesus said the kingdom of God is like a pearl that is so amazing, a merchant would trade everything else he has to possess it. Jesus also compared the kingdom to a mustard seed: "the smallest of all the seeds, but when it has grown it is the greatest of shrubs" (Matthew 13:32). People were anticipating a future time when God would set up his kingdom on earth, reigning over all the nations. Jesus stressed that God's kingdom wasn't just a "there and then," it was a "here and now." God's kingdom is wherever and whenever people honor him as their king. When we pray for his kingdom to come, we raise his flag now in our hearts.

Some people are confused by the phrase "your will be done." Doesn't God do what he wants, anyway? Maybe so, but as we pray this, we are communicating our compliance. We are saying, "We want what you want, Lord." It's a commitment to live the way God wants us to live.

As the Israelites wandered the desert in Moses' day, they knew all about daily bread. God sent manna from heaven each day to sustain them. But if someone tried to hoard any manna, it quickly spoiled. They had to trust God to provide for them each day. Nowadays, if you're thoroughly insured and securely invested, you might miss out on the joy of appreciating God's daily provision. But problems still arise, alerting us to our need for God in our lives. Jesus says we should ask God for what we need.

Confession is also part of this model prayer, but there's a catch. We ask God to forgive our debts (or trespasses), but we are expected to offer forgiveness to others. Jesus told a story about a servant who was forgiven a debt of millions of dollars but then demanded payment of a few dollars from someone else. That's not the way it's supposed to work. Forgiven people are expected to forgive others. It's a change of heart. Once you understand how much God has forgiven you, your heart melts in mercy toward others.

This prayer concludes with a plea for deliverance from temptation ("the time of trial") and from evil. Basically, we don't want to face trials, but if we do, we don't want evil to triumph over us. The first request is sometimes denied. Believers will face trials. Just two chapters earlier, we find Jesus being led into temptation by the Spirit (Matthew 4:1), and yet he was given strength to overcome it. There is no shame in praying to avoid difficult times, but we must recognize that often God uses them to help us grow. In the Garden of Gethsemane, Jesus prayed that the time of trial would be removed. It wasn't. But then he invoked another part of the Lord's Prayer when he said, "Your will be done" (Mark 14:36). When we do face trials, we can be assured that God is right there with us.

CHAPTER THREE

PRAYERS

for

HELP

BREAKFAST WITH GOD
Psalm 143:8

Let me hear of your steadfast love in the morning, for in you I put my trust. Teach me the way I should go, for to you I lift up my soul.

A VITAMIN FOR THE SOUL

THE FIRST THING we think about in the morning should be the love of God. If we start by remembering that he loves us, we will trust him. And then we will do his will. Have you had your morning psalm? Serve it up before breakfast, and taste the goodness of God. Everything goes down better after that. Think of it as a vitamin for the soul, fortifying your desire to spend your day serving our Lord.

PICTURING THE LORD
Saint Colomba

My dearest Lord,
Be thou a bright flame before me,

Be thou a guiding star above me,
Be thou a smooth path beneath me,
Be thou a kindly shepherd behind me,
Today and for evermore.

HE WILL NEVER LOSE US

WITH THE DAWNING of each new day, we need courage to take every new step in the walk of faith. Thankfully, we have God's bright guidance, his smooth pathways, and his gentle leadership.

Colomba must have known these things well. He was an Irish missionary who lived from 521 to 597. He journeyed to share the love of God with villagers who lived off the coast of Scotland on the island of Iona. Through Colomba's missionary work, even a king, the king of the Picts, felt his heart warmed by the gospel message and became a Christian.

In this prayer Colomba depicted the Lord using four images—a flame, a star, a path, and a shepherd. What modern pictures or similes would you use for your own relationship with the Lord? For most of us, even in our thoroughly modern situations, the image of a shepherd still speaks of the things we most need and want in our daily lives. For so often we feel like vulnerable sheep walking along paths that can be rocky and dangerous.

Yet, as Colomba affirms, if we stumble or lose our way, like a shepherd of infinite goodwill, our Shepherd picks us up and puts us back on the path. Therefore, let us be assured: *Even if we lose faith for a while, he will never lose us.*

Do Not Forget Me
Jacob Astley

O Lord! Thou knowest how busy I must be this day: if I forget thee, do not thou forget me.

Take Time to Pray

WE ALL LEAD busy lives, and we often forget or do not take the time to pray. We forget to turn to God when we are troubled; we forget that he can help us when we are feeling overwhelmed. We also forget to give thanks; we forget to acknowledge God as the source of all that is good in our lives.

Sir Jacob Astley wrote this brief but powerful prayer before he was to partake in the Battle of Edgehill during the English Civil War. No doubt Astley desired the assurance that God would be watching over him during the battle, just as we desire the assurance that God will be with us when we feel weak or frightened. Although we may sometimes forget God, we can be assured that God is always watching over us; he will never forget us.

THE NEW MAN
Book of Common Prayer

O merciful God, grant that the old Adam in this child may be so buried, that the new man may be raised up in him.

A PURE SPIRIT

THIS SIMPLE yet profound baptism prayer asks God to take away the sinner within us and replace it with a pure and innocent spirit. The "old Adam" is the old human nature, which is prone to sin and selfishness. The "new man" is the new nature, which seeks to please God and be like Christ.

When children are baptized, we ask that they be born anew in the Holy Spirit, but this prayer can be profoundly effective even for adults struggling to turn away from evil and sinful temptations.

THY WILL BE DONE
Psalm 143:1, 8–11

Hear my prayer, O Lord; give ear to my supplications in your faithfulness; answer me in your righteousness. . . .

Let me hear of your steadfast love in the morning, for in you I put my trust. Teach me the way I should go, for to you I lift up my soul.

Save me, O Lord, from my enemies; I have fled to you for refuge. Teach me to do your will, for you are my God. Let your good spirit lead me on a level path.

For your name's sake, O Lord, preserve my life. In your righteousness bring me out of trouble.

LET THE SPIRIT LEAD

SØREN KIERKEGAARD once said, "Prayer does not change God, but it changes the one who prays." Sincere prayer does this by changing our "my will be done" into "thy will be done," even as Christ himself taught us to pray in the Lord's Prayer.

Eventually we all have to pray a prayer like the one the psalmist prayed. It is a prayer for God to teach us the way we should go, to teach us to do his will, and to let his good Spirit lead us on a level path.

The Lord is always eager to do this, and when we pray this way, the Holy Spirit teaches us how to love God and to love others. Now that's a life-changing prayer.

IN CHRIST'S FOOTSTEPS
St. Francis of Assisi

Almighty, eternal, just and merciful God, grant us the desire to do only what pleases you, and the strength to do only what you command. Cleanse our souls, enlighten our minds, and inflame our hearts with your Holy Spirit, that we may follow in the footsteps of your beloved Son, Jesus Christ.

ASK AND FOLLOW

FRANCIS OF ASSISI is usually associated with two particular prayers: "The Peace Prayer of St. Francis" and "Brother Sun, Sister Moon." In this prayer, however, he shares more of his insight about Christ. He offers us a wonderful opportunity to reconnect with the Holy Spirit, which enlightens us in how to faithfully walk with Jesus Christ.

When we make the choice to live according to God's will, we know that we will also be given the fortitude and courage needed to change what is not working in our lives. God never gives us an opportunity without also providing us with a way to make it work. Nor does God ever give us a command we are not empowered to obey. If we truly want to change our lives, all we have to do is ask and then follow the path that the Spirit paves for us.

OUR RESTLESS HEARTS
St. Augustine

Thou hast made us for Thyself,
And our hearts are restless
until they rest in Thee.

SECURITY IN GOD

AUGUSTINE WAS BORN into humble circumstances. Yet, he went on to become Bishop of Hippo in Africa for parts of the fourth and fifth centuries. He was also considered the foremost Christian thinker for a thousand years between the apostle Paul and the theologian Thomas Aquinas.

As a young man, Augustine wrote *Confessions*, a collection of personal memoirs that narrated his search for earthly satisfaction. His experiences often resulted in a guilty conscience, causing Augustine much distress. His life changed radically, however, when he realized that his spiritual restlessness would continue until he finally gave his heart to a peaceful rest in God.

Augustine's prayer has life-changing potential for us today. By seeing our restlessness as a natural part of life, we come to a greater reality: There is more to existence than what we see. Our anxieties can push us to reflect on our true purposes in life and to surrender to God. We can use our daily agitation to establish more meaningful priorities and develop and strengthen our relationship with God. Like Augustine, we, too, can arrive at a rest in God as the Satisfier of our souls.

Later in life, Augustine penned *The City of God*, which laid out a vision of God's will and ways in human society. He wrote it during a time when his own home in North Africa stood on the brink of terrorist attack. Thus, in his day and in ours, the truth remains: God is the ultimate source of our security.

A Prayerful Journey
Psalm 121:5–8

The Lord is your keeper; the Lord is your shade at your right hand. The sun shall not strike you by day, nor the moon by night.

The Lord will keep you from all evil; he will keep your life. The Lord will keep your going out and your coming in from this time on and forevermore.

An Excellent Promise

THIS ANCIENT HEBREW prayer of pilgrimage is about the specific fears of travelers. Saying this prayer as a protective cover, they believed the Lord would keep them from sunstroke on the hot dusty roads and from being moonstruck, which they thought caused insanity.

Despite their superstition, this prayer can be an appropriate prayer for us, for it rightfully assumes an excellent promise: Truly the Lord will keep us. All we have to do is trust that he loves us and will always protect us—then we will have no reason to worry.

GOD'S LOVING WILL
St. Ignatius

Take, O Lord, and receive my entire liberty, my memory, my understanding and my whole will. All that I am and all that I possess You have given me. I surrender it all to You to be disposed of according to Your will. Give me only Your love and Your grace; with these I will be rich enough, and will desire nothing more.

FOR THE GREATER GLORY OF GOD

WHILE INIGO DE LOYOLA was recuperating from a severe leg injury, he underwent a life-changing experience. For several weeks, he had been cloistered in a castle, where out of sheer boredom he picked up a book on the life of Christ and Christian saints. As he read, he felt a strong connection with the saints and their lives of devotion to Christ.

"Ignatius," as he would become known, eventually met with the Pope, traveled to the Holy Land on pilgrimage, and studied Latin in Barcelona, where he became a priest. So zealous was Ignatius in his desire to teach others how to pray, the Inquisition jailed him for 42 days.

Ignatius founded the Society of Jesus, whose motto is *Ad Majorem Dei Gloriam*; it means "for the greater glory of God." Everything Ignatius did was for the love of God; this was the secret to his success and the reason for his joy.

Ignatius became a teacher and worked to establish Jesuit schools and universities all over the world. He was also a gifted spiritual writer. To this day, Christians seeking to express their love for the Lord often recite his prayers.

This particular prayer is one of surrender—of completely giving oneself over to God's will and asking only for his love and grace in return. How Ignatius must have felt, loving God so strongly and feeling so strongly loved in return! This prayer reminds us that God's love is available to each of us; we need only to ask for it.

From Jesus, we learn that we should desire only the kingdom of God because everything else we need will be given to us once we enter the kingdom. What Ignatius teaches us through this prayer is very similar: Once we receive the glory of God's loving grace, we will desire nothing more; we will have everything.

God's love is worth more than all the riches in the world; it is the most precious gift we could receive. To recognize, as Ignatius did, that all we are is because of God is a wisdom the soul longs for; it makes the soul complete. To give ourselves over to this wisdom and let it guide our lives is to be who God intended us to be.

SONG FOR A SON
1 Samuel 2:1-10

Hannah prayed and said, "My heart exults in the Lord; my strength is exalted in my God. My mouth derides my enemies, because I rejoice in my victory. There is no Holy One like the Lord, no one besides you; there is no Rock like our God. Talk no more so very proudly, let not arrogance come from your mouth; for the Lord is a God of knowledge, and by him actions are weighed. The bows of the mighty are broken, but the feeble gird on strength. Those who were full have hired themselves out for bread, but those who were hungry are fat with spoil. The barren has borne seven, but she who has many children is forlorn. The Lord kills and brings to life; he brings down to Sheol and raises up. The Lord makes poor and makes rich; he brings low, he also exalts. He raises up the poor from the dust; he lifts the needy from the ash heap, to make them sit with princes and inherit a seat of honor. For the pillars of the earth are the Lord's, and on them he has set the world. He will guard the feet of his faithful ones, but the wicked shall be cut off in darkness; for not by might does one prevail. The Lord! His adversaries shall be shattered; the Most High will thunder in heaven. The Lord will judge the ends of the earth; he *will give strength to his king, and exalt the power of his anointed."*

OVERCOMING OBSTACLES THROUGH PRAYER

Her biological clock was ticking, and Hannah wanted a child. Her husband, Elkanah, was not rushing her; he was happy just to have her as his wife. Also, his other wife, Peninnah, had children already, and he was not in a hurry to have more. But Hannah was. Peninnah constantly teased her about her inability to conceive, often provoking Hannah to tears.

So one day when Hannah was "deeply distressed... and wept bitterly" (1 Samuel 1:10), she made a vow. If God would give her a son, she would give that son back to God. She would allow him to be raised as a Nazirite, someone specially dedicated to God. She would give him to the priest to raise, letting the boy grow up in the tabernacle.

The priest, Eli, saw Hannah praying silently, and at first he thought she must be drunk. Her lips moved, but no sound was made. She replied that she was deeply troubled. "I have been pouring out my soul before the Lord" (1 Samuel 1:15). The priest blessed her, adding his prayer that her prayer would be answered.

It was. She gave birth to a son and named him Samuel. When the boy was about three years old, she brought him to the tabernacle and presented him to Eli, saying, "I am the woman who was standing here in your presence, praying to the Lord. For this child I prayed; and the Lord has granted me the petition that I made to him. Therefore I have lent him to the Lord" (1 Samuel 1:26–28). And then Hannah offered her prayer-song of praise.

THE JOY OF ANSWERED PRAYER

HANNAH'S PRAYER is one of genuine joy and adoration for God. She thanks God for listening to those who pray and helping those who admit their need for him. How often do we ask God to deliver us from a situation and then fail to give him thanks and praise when our request is granted? Almost four years after God answered her prayer to conceive, Hannah was still uttering thanks.

At first glance, Hannah's prayer-song might seem out of place. It's a social commentary. She's talking about "victory" and "enemies" and God breaking the "bows of the mighty." David the soldier might have written something like this, but Hannah? Yet we should consider her situation. Barrenness was a disgrace for women in her culture; Hannah was even teased by a woman who was "rich" with children. Hannah asked God to conquer her barrenness, and he did. By turning to the Lord, Hannah saw herself exalted into the state of motherhood.

One beautiful aspect of this song is that it shows God working in everyday life. If you read Joshua and Judges, you might get the idea that God only cares about warfare. He helps generals, armies, and nations. But Hannah teaches us that God also grants victory to a woman who wants a baby. He is continually exalting the poor, challenging the rich, and guarding the feet of the faithful—not just in the front-page news of nations and armies, but in the day-to-day problems of families as well.

Hannah's prayer is very similar to another song of exaltation, Mary's Magnificat (Luke 1:46–55). Both use the occasion of motherhood to sing about the wonderful ways that God works. Both deal with how God brings down kings and lifts the lowly. And in both cases, God brings a special person into the world: Jesus and Samuel.

The role of Jesus in achieving God's purposes is obvious. But Samuel, Hannah's son, also played a pivotal role in history. He brought order to chaos during the time of the judges. When King Saul became too proud, Samuel announced that the throne would be taken away. And Samuel found the new king tending sheep in Bethlehem: a lowly herder named David. So Hannah's prayer also hints at the kind of life her son would have.

There's an old Sunday school saying: "You're never too little to be used by God, but he can't use you if you're too big." Hannah captures this simple, wonderful truth in her song. Hannah acknowledges that "not by might does one prevail" (1 Samuel 2:9), but we will certainly prevail if we put our trust in God.

Even in her weakness, Hannah was still able to admit and be comforted by her dependence on God. In our self-reliant, do-it-yourself, individualistic world, it can be hard to admit that we need God. But a child who wanders from a parent will soon become scared and hungry and seek comfort and food; in the same way, we grow weak when we stray from God. He calls us back as a parent would, letting us know we can look to him to provide strength and nourishment in all that we do.

Showdown on Mount Carmel
1 Kings 18:36–37

The prophet Elijah came near and said, "O Lord, God of Abraham, Isaac, and Israel, let it be known this day that you are God in Israel, that I am your servant, and that I have done all these things at your bidding. Answer me, O Lord, answer me, so that this people may know that you, O Lord, are God, and that you have turned their hearts back."

A Demonstration of God's Power

THE SCENE must have been electric. These days it would be covered live on all the networks, hyped around the clock as the day approached. The prophet Elijah, the mysterious man from the wrong side of the river, was challenging the royal prophets to a duel on Mount Carmel. Each side would prepare a bull for sacrifice upon an altar and then call their god to rain down fire from heaven to consume it.

King Ahab and Queen Jezebel had led the Israelites away from their traditional beliefs and into the worship of regional fertility gods, primarily the sky-god Baal. Elijah had spoken courageously against this, but sometimes he felt like he was the only one who did so. On Mount Carmel, it was 450 against one. "Then you call on the name of your god and I will call on the name of the Lord; the god who answers by fire is indeed God" (1 Kings 18:24), Elijah challenged, as he reviewed the rules of this showdown.

The Baal-worshipers started early in the morning and worked all day, readying the sacrifice and calling out to their deity. At noon, Elijah began to add some fun to the proceedings, urging them to pray louder, suggesting that Baal might be off traveling or catching a nap. Desperately, the royal prophets began to cut themselves with swords, letting their blood gush over them. At the end of the day,

Scripture records the score: Baal had supplied "no voice, no answer, and no response" (1 Kings 18:29).

Rebuilding the broken altar, Elijah prepared the sacrifice and poured water over the entire altar, filling a trench he had dug around it. There would be no room for questions about this miracle. Then he prayed this prayer. The Bible says, "Then the fire of the Lord fell and consumed the burnt offering, the wood, the stones, and the dust, and even licked up the water that was in the trench" (1 Kings 18:38). Public opinion immediately swayed back to Elijah's God. The prayer had been answered.

SHORT AND STEEP

AFTER HIS OPPONENTS called on their god all day, Elijah spoke two simple sentences to his God. Sometimes people think they have to use flowery words or pious phrases, going on and on about why God should answer their prayers. But all those words become babble to God. Jesus chided the Gentiles who thought God would hear them because they talked a lot (Matthew 6:7). God prefers the plain, honest words of our hearts. As Proverbs 17:27–28 says, "One who spares words is knowledgeable."

Notice also how Elijah raised the stakes in this encounter. By pouring water on the sacrifice, he made it even harder for fire to consume it. But he knew God wouldn't blink an eye at that challenge. Elijah had complete confidence in God's power.

This doesn't mean that we should randomly demand outrageous miracles from God. Many kids (and even a few adults) have tested Jesus' teachings about faith moving mountains by ordering Mount Everest to relocate to Australia. That misses the point. We need to be so in touch with God that we know which mountains he wants to move. That's what faith does for you, and that's exactly what Elijah had. Who do you think sent him to Mount Carmel to begin with?

The prayer itself is inspiring. Elijah invokes the God of the patriarchs, using Jacob's alternate name, Israel, because it was also the name of the nation Elijah was summoning back to God. He wants the Lord to demonstrate two things: God's power and the validity of Elijah's ministry. That might seem self-serving, but Elijah was playing a key role in this drama. Many Israelites probably knew the Lord as "Elijah's God." In fact, Elijah's name means "The Lord (Jah, God's personal name) is my God (Eli)." God was working through Elijah to turn the hearts of the people back to him.

In the same way, we might find ourselves representing God in front of neighbors and friends. We won't be offering bulls on altars in the backyard, but we might speak up for the Lord in various ways. Our culture worships things such as money, pleasure, beauty, and sports. When God asks us to challenge these idols, we can surely look to him for support.

Yet the ultimate goal of Elijah's prayer was not personal pride but the return of Israel to God. As Jesus explained to his followers, God desires the return of his lost people as a father desires the return of a lost child (Luke 15:11–32). You can't read very far in Scripture without hearing this message loud and clear. He still awaits our return today. We can confidently pray that God will turn the hearts of his people to him.

MY BROTHER'S KEEPER
Genesis 32:9–12

God of my father Abraham and God of my father Isaac, O Lord who said to me, "Return to your country and to your kindred, and I
will do you good," I am not worthy of the least of all the steadfast love and all the faithfulness that you have shown to your servant, for with only my staff I crossed this Jordan; and now I have become two companies. Deliver me, please, from the hand
of my brother, from the hand of Esau, for I am afraid of him; he may come and kill us all, the

mothers with the children. Yet you have said, "I will surely do you good, and make your offspring as the sand of the sea, which cannot be counted because of their number."

PRAYING FOR DELIVERANCE

TALK ABOUT dysfunctional families! First, Jacob cheated his older brother, Esau, out of the family inheritance. Then, with the help of his mother, he disguised himself as Esau and received the sacred blessing from their blind and dying father. When Esau discovered what Jacob had done, he vowed to kill him once their father died. Hearing of this plan, Jacob fled and avoided Esau for 20 years.

During that time, Jacob had a few new adventures, such as getting married—twice—and fathering a caravan of kids. But his father-in-law was just as much of a trickster as he was, so Jacob eventually decided to move back to his homeland. By this time he was a wealthy man, with flocks and herds and servants (and, of course, all those children). But along the journey he received word that Esau was coming to meet him with an army of 400 men. This made Jacob more than a little nervous.

He didn't have a lot of time. Jacob quickly split his possessions and his family into two traveling parties so that if one group was attacked, the other could escape. Then he launched his frantic and desperate plea for God's protection.

The prayer is both comical and touching. Jacob begins by reminding God that he is only in this predicament because he followed God's will—as if to say, "You're the one who got me into this mess, and you told me that everything would be fine if I listened to you." That's Jacob, always seeking an upper hand in negotiations.

But then Jacob offers thanks to God for the blessings he has received at his hand. There is a sense of genuine gratitude and adoration as Jacob admits that he had nothing when he crossed the Jordan River, and now everything that he has he owes to God. He knows in his heart that God is in control, but his head can't stop worrying about his angry brother approaching with that battalion.

HONEST AND FAITHFUL

JACOB IS HARDLY a paragon of virtue. As we read the stories in Genesis about him, he often appears selfish, dishonest, and mischievous. And still there is a lot we can learn from him. Most of all, he keeps in touch with God. This is the man who wrestled with God one night in a dream. That could be a picture of Jacob's entire life. He didn't always make the right moves, but he never let go of God. For imperfect folks like us, that's a pretty good lesson to learn.

And this prayer gives us an interesting combination of honesty and fragile faith. Sometimes we sacrifice honesty for faith. For example, Jacob could have acted as if he was not scared of his advancing brother. He could have said, "God, I know that everything will be all right. I have complete faith in you." But that wouldn't have been honest. Instead, Jacob is both honest and faithful, admitting "I am afraid of [Esau]," but still clinging to God's promise to do good for him. Jacob is truly scared, but that does not mean that he thinks God will let him down. When we pray about a situation—whether it's financial, work-related, or involving a relationship—we should be honest with God about our fears and look realistically at the possible outcomes. But we should also trust that God will get us through the situation, often with better results than we could have imagined.

That's what happened to Jacob. When they finally met, Esau ran and hugged him. It was a time of rejoicing. God did keep his promises, as he always does.

I AM NOT WORTHY
Book of Common Prayer

I am not worthy, Holy Lord,
That Thou shouldst come to me:
Speak but the Word, one gracious Word,
Can set the sinner free.

I am not worthy: cold and bare
The lodging of my soul:
How canst Thou deign to enter there?
Lord, speak and make me whole.

FAITH IS THE KEY

WHEN JESUS entered Capernaum, a Centurion approached him and appealed for a dying slave he deeply cared about. Being a Roman soldier, however, the Centurion did not feel worthy of Jesus' attention. In fact, he said to the Lord, "I am not worthy... but only speak the word, and let my servant be healed" (Luke 7:6–7).

This simple prayer of faith and belief so impressed Jesus that he turned to the crowd of witnesses and declared, "I tell you, not even in Israel have I found such faith" (Luke 7:9). Jesus then healed the slave.

Several times Jesus tried to tell his followers that faith was the key to joy and miracles, but not many of them truly understood. It took a Roman soldier, a natural enemy of the Jews, to have the kind of faith Jesus was talking about.

Even though we are sinners, Christ still loves us. Even when we are weak and afraid, Christ still loves us. In fact, nothing we can do can cause us to fall out of Christ's favor if we have sincere faith in him. If we go before Jesus with a humble, believing heart, we will be given a multitude of blessings in return. This is wonderful news for those times when we feel as though we don't even deserve what we have already been given.

Jesus is trying to tell us that we will receive more, much more. In fact, we will receive the kingdom of God. Yet, something is first required of us, as the Centurion realized: We must ask; we must knock upon the door; and we must believe. Then, Jesus will answer.

TURN US AGAIN
Psalm 80:3–7 NLT

Turn us again to yourself, O God. Make your face shine down upon us. Only then will we be saved.

O LORD God Almighty, how long will you be angry and reject our prayers? You have fed us with sorrow and made us drink tears by the bucketful. You have made us the scorn of neighboring nations. Our enemies treat us as a joke.

Turn us again to yourself, O God Almighty. Make your face shine down upon us. Only then will we be saved.

A LIGHT FOR THE WORLD

GOD IS SO BRIGHT that he did not even want Moses to look at him. Once, when he passed by Moses, Moses could see only his back. Moses' own face then became so radiant that he had to wear a veil when he talked with the people.

After that, and after a thousand failures, the people wanted to see God's face again. They prayed, "Turn us again to yourself, O God. Make your face shine down upon us. Only then will we be saved." It's a request repeated seven times in the Book of Psalms. It's a request we should repeat ourselves, allowing the light of his glory to make our faces to shine. A life of faith transforms our countenance so that we mirror the light of God in a dark world.

Indeed, Paul said that God made his light shine "in our hearts to give the light of the knowledge of the glory of God in the face of Jesus Christ" (2 Corinthians 4:6).

DAVID'S LAMENT
Psalm 22:6–11 NLT

But I am a worm and not a man. I am scorned and despised by all! Everyone who sees me mocks me. They sneer and shake their heads, saying, "Is this the one who relies on the Lord? Then let the Lord save him! If the Lord loves him so much, let the Lord rescue him!"

Yet you brought me safely from my mother's womb and led me to trust you when I was a nursing infant. I was thrust upon you at my birth. You have been my God from the moment I was born. Do not stay so far from me, for trouble is near, and no one else can help me.

UNWAVERING FAITH

DAVID IS the author of this prayer, which mentions how people often ridiculed him mercilessly. His brothers laughed at him when he said he would kill the giant Goliath, and the giant mocked him before they battled. Nevertheless, David knew that God would deliver him. David held this assurance throughout his life, even when he fled his own palace because his son, Absalom, tried to usurp the throne. And, in each case, God stood with him.

Most of us will never fight a giant or a bear—at least not the kind with arms and legs—but we will encounter immense problems, and some people will expect us to fail. That's when we should say this prayer of surrender to the Lord: "You have been my God from the moment I was born. Do not stay so far from me, for trouble is near, and no one else can help me."

PRECIOUS LORD, TAKE MY HAND
Thomas Andrew Dorsey

Precious Lord, take my hand,
Lead me on, let me stand,
I am tired, I am weak, I am worn;
Thru the storm, thru the night,
Lead me on to the light,
Take my hand, precious Lord,
Lead me home.
When the darkness appears and the night
draws near,
And the day is past and gone,
At the river I stand,
Guide my feet, hold my hand;
Take my hand, precious Lord,
Lead me home.

FIND COMFORT IN THE LORD

THOMAS DORSEY started his career playing backup for famous blues singers. Then, in the 1920s, he began to write songs about faith. A self-taught pianist, his interests switched back and forth from bawdy blues lyrics to church choral music until 1932, when his wife Nettie died in child-birth. To console himself he wrote this famous prayer-song, "Precious Lord, Take My Hand."

From then on, he never turned back from writing Christian music. He eventually became known as the "Father of Gospel Music." In fact, he coined the term "gospel music" for songs of worship with the bounce and rhythm of early blues and jazz. He composed more than 1,000 gospel songs before his death in 1991. One of those songs was "Peace in the Valley," which earned gold records for both Elvis Presley and Red Foley.

"Precious Lord, Take My Hand" turned out to be the most famous of his hymns. It has encouraged millions to find comfort in the Lord's guidance and care. As only he can, the Lord used Dorsey's dark time to lead others to the light.

Toward Jerusalem
Amy Carmichael

Father, hear us, we are praying.
Hear the words our hearts are saying.
We are praying for our children.
Keep them from the powers of evil,

from the secret hidden peril,
from the whirlpool that would suck them,
from the treacherous quicksand, pluck them.
From the worldling's hollow gladness,
from the sting of faithless sadness,
Holy Father, save our children.
Through life's troubled waters steer them,
through life's bitter battle cheer them,
Father, Father, be Thou near them.
Read the language of our longing,
read the wordless pleadings thronging,
Holy Father, for our children.
And wherever they may bide,
lead them home at eventide.

SAVE OUR CHILDREN

A LOT OF PEOPLE pray for children. Amy Carmichael was one of them, but she did more than just pray for them. Once, she had a vision of Jesus weeping and praying for all the children of the world, and this changed her life forever. As a missionary in India, she had seen young girls being sold as temple prostitutes, and she decided to do something about it.

She began to buy the young girls herself—even against the opposition of townspeople and authorities—in order to rescue them. Any girl who escaped from the temple was welcomed at the home and school she established, and before her death in 1951, she had provided a new life for more than 1,000 children. Amy Carmichael certainly followed the teaching of the apostle James: "We are made right with God by what we do, not by faith alone" (James 2:24).

This teaching and the example of Amy Carmichael can change us as well; we can love the children in our lives with prayer *and* action.

CHRIST'S OWN PRAYER
John 17:1, 11–21

Jesus looked up to heaven and said . . . "Father, the time has come. Glorify your Son so he can give glory back to you. Now I am departing the world; I am leaving them behind and coming to you. Holy Father, keep them and care for them—all those you have given me—so that they will be united just as we are. During my time here, I have kept them safe. I guarded them so that not one was lost, except the one headed for destruction, as the Scriptures foretold. And now I am coming to you. I have told them many things while I was with them so they would be filled with my joy. I have given them your word. And the world hates them because they do not belong to the world, just as I do not.

I'm not asking you to take them out of the world, but to keep them safe from the evil one. They are not part of this world any more than I am. Make them pure and holy by teaching them your words of truth. As you sent me into the world, I am sending them into the world. And I give myself entirely to you so they also might be entirely yours.

I am praying not only for these disciples but also for all who will ever believe in me because of their testimony. My prayer for all of them is that they will be one, just as you and I are one, Father—that just as you are in me and I am in you, so they will be in us, and the world will believe you sent me."

PROTECT THEM

THIS WONDERFUL, comforting passage of Scripture is often called the *real* Lord's prayer. The traditional prayer—the one we recite in church—is one Christ prayed when the disciples asked him to teach them to pray. It is a powerful model of how we should pray and what we should pray for. This is Christ's own prayer, however, offered the night he was betrayed. It is an intimate, personal prayer, one which shows his love for his disciples, as well as for us.

Basically, Jesus asked his heavenly Father to protect his disciples. He also, though, asked God to protect those who will believe in him through the testimony of his disciples—in other words, us. Yet, while it is important enough that we are protected, the prayer is more important for what it says about Jesus' heart. On the eve of his own death, he was thinking of us, and he wanted us to have three very important things.

First, Jesus wanted us to have unity. He prayed, "Keep them and care for them . . . so that they will be united just as we are." Throughout his life Jesus had a deep and powerful unity with his heavenly Father, and he wanted us to have that unity with each other as well as with himself and the Father. "My prayer for all of them is that they will be one, just as you and I are one, Father," he prayed, "that just as you are in me and I am in you, so they will be in us, and the world will believe you sent me."

Another thing Jesus wanted us to have was truth and purpose. The unity that he desires for us is based on a common message and a common mission. He has given us the Father's words, and now he sends us out to share those words with others. They are words of truth, he says, words that sanctify us, setting us apart for noble work.

What Jesus seemed to want the most was for us to have his joy. In fact, he says that's why he prayed this prayer "in the earth," while he was still with his disciples. His was an uncommon joy—one he had in his darkest hour—because he was one with the Father and obedient to the Father's word. This third thing Jesus wanted for us we can have only when we treasure our oneness and his word.

That was a strange night for the disciples, filled with strange events and strange emotions. Jesus washed their feet and transformed the ancient Passover feast into the Eucharist, or the Lord's Supper. The room was filled with tension, and the danger was great, but then Jesus prayed this tender, gracious prayer to comfort them.

And, 2000 years later, this prayer brings all of us great comfort, too.

THY WILL BE DONE
Mark 14:36

He said, "Abba, Father, for you all things are possible; remove this cup from me; yet, not what I want, but what you want."

NOT MY WILL . . .

I⸀T WAS the last night before the crucifixion. Jesus enjoyed the Passover meal with his disciples and then took them to a secluded place on the Mount of Olives, the Garden of Gethsemane. The gospel of Mark says that Jesus "began to be distressed and agitated" (Mark 14:33). He left his disci-

ples, urging them to stay awake and went off by himself
to pray.

Jesus had plenty to be distressed and agitated about. In the
three years of his ministry, he had made enemies among
the religious elite. Though he had been warned not to make
this Passover trip to Jerusalem, he insisted. He had told his
disciples that a cross awaited him, and yet he had entered
the city to triumphal shouts. He had faced off against the
moneychangers in the temple, and in those last days he
had continued his public teaching.

It seemed that as long as he was in public the authorities
wouldn't arrest him, fearing a reaction by the people. They
needed to find him alone, or with only his disciples, so
they could take him without causing a scene.

But Jesus dodged them effectively for a few days. That's
why they needed Judas to lead the way to him. Even in
planning the site of the Last Supper, Jesus employed
secrecy, telling some disciples to meet a mysterious man
carrying water and to follow him home. Perhaps that was
so Judas would not know in advance where they'd be din-
ing. Jesus wanted those last precious hours with his
friends.

Finally, he was in the garden, begging his disciples to stay
awake—probably for their own protection. He might have
already seen the train of torches snaking through the valley and up the mountain—Judas leading the temple guard

to arrest him. Distressed and agitated? You would have been, too.

A Deep Intimacy

IN THIS TIME of crisis, he turned to his Father in prayer. "Abba, Father," he began, and already we get a sense of their relationship. Abba is an Aramaic word used by children. The best English translation is something like "Daddy." There was a deep intimacy between Father and Son.

We take for granted the idea of God as Father, but actually it seldom appears in the Old Testament. The psalmist likens God to a father who cares for his children (Psalm 103:13), and has God calling the Israelite king (and the coming Messiah) his Son (Psalm 2:7).

But Jesus was one step ahead when he invited his followers to address God as "our Father" and in his repeated references to "the Father in heaven." Yet the word Abba makes it clear that he's not just talking about "Our Father" but "my Father." More accurately, he means "my Daddy." Whatever else he prays in this situation, it's based on this tight-knit relationship.

Jesus continues his prayer in much the same way: "Abba, you're the best. All things are possible for you. God can do anything." Amazingly, Jesus was suggesting that there might be some other way to fulfill God's plan, a way that wouldn't involve his cruel crucifixion. At least he was hoping there might be.

In our lives, we often get distressed and agitated by matters that are beyond our control. It helps to realize that God is not locked into our limitations. We assume there are, maybe, two or three possible outcomes, each equally bad. But God has the power to do a million amazing things beyond what we ask or even think.

In the garden, Jesus went on to ask for what he wanted. Could he get through this without having to drink the cup of suffering? Obviously, he knew there was great pain ahead—physical and spiritual. Who can blame him for wanting to avoid it, if possible?

Ultimately, Jesus offered his submission. After presenting his own "will"—what he wanted to happen—he bowed to his Father's will. As Matthew records it, "Thy will be done."

A HOLY HEART
St. Thomas More

*Lord, grant me a holy heart
that sees always what is fine and pure*

and is not frightened at the sight of sin
but creates order wherever it goes.
Grant me a heart that knows nothing of boredom,
Weeping and sighing.
Let me not be too concerned
with the bothersome thing I call "myself."
Lord, give me a sense of humor
And I will find happiness in life and profit for others.

COMPLETE SURRENDER TO GOD

CONVICTIONS WERE COSTLY in the days of Thomas More (1478–1535). Remaining true to his Christian heritage, he refused to support the edicts of Henry VIII, king of England, because they were contrary to the teachings of Christ. Thus, More was eventually placed in the Tower of London, accused of treason, and beheaded.

His prayer for a holy heart might well have been written during his stay in prison while he awaited his death. Any of us who feel imprisoned by a current crisis could pray these words along with More—that we not be overwhelmed with weeping and sighing but instead surrender ourselves totally to the God who loves us.

It is a great compliment to More's character that, while he was surely experiencing the worst anxiety, he nevertheless prayed to be less concerned with himself—a "bothersome thing." In this regard, note the unselfish sentiments that fill his final letter, written to his daughter Margaret on July 5, 1535, the day before he was executed: "Our Lord bless you, good daughter, and your good husband, and your little boy, and all yours, and all my children, and all my god-children and all our friends. . . . I cumber you, good Margaret, much, but I would be sorry if it should be any longer than to-morrow . . . and therefore, to-morrow long I to go to God. It were a day very meet and convenient for me."

More's surrender to God was complete in every way.

THE BLESSING OF NEED
Charles Spurgeon

Lord, I am in need, be pleased to supply me; but, meanwhile, if you do not, I believe it is better for me to be in need, and so I praise you for my necessity while I ask you to supply it. I glory in my infirmity, even while I ask you to overcome it. I bless you for my affliction even while I ask you to help me in it and to rescue me out of it.

CONFIDENCE IN GOD'S WILL

THE 19TH-CENTURY British pastor Charles Spurgeon was called "The Prince of Preachers." He is also the author of a 63-volume collection of sermons; this is the largest set of books by a single writer in the history of Christianity. He was known as a humble person with a sense of humor and a love for the downcast of society.

Both Spurgeon and his wife, Susanna, suffered from health problems. In his case, it was severe gout. He often preached in great pain, and he died at the early age of 58. It is no wonder, then, that in this prayer he asked for help with his infirmity. What is surprising is that he gloried in it and blessed God for it!

Spurgeon had absolute confidence in God; he believed that even though the reason behind it was beyond his comprehension, his infirmity was part of God's plan for his life, so it must be good. Trusting in God's will as Spurgeon did would transform our lives—and perhaps the lives of those around us, too.

THE SEA OF FAITH
Henri Nouwen

O Lord, sea of love and goodness, let me not fear too much the storms and winds of my daily life, and let me know that there is ebb and flow but that the sea remains the sea.

BE NOT AFRAID

BATTLING THE STORMY times in our lives can certainly be frightening. Henri Nouwen, a priest who gave up a promising clerical career to work in a home for the mentally challenged, must often have faced the cruel waves of discouragement. For him, as for us, it's only natural to pray for deliverance from fear.

Yet, if we keep in mind that the storms we face are no different from the storms people have always faced, we can rest assured in the knowledge that God is always with us, guiding us to just the right destination.

HE HEARS YOU
Lamentations 3:52–58

Those who were my enemies without cause have hunted me like a bird; they flung me alive into a pit and hurled stones on me; water closed over my head; I said, "I am lost." I called on your name, O Lord, from the depths of the pit; you heard my plea, "Do not close your ear to my cry for help, but give me relief!" You came near when I called on you; you said, "Do not fear!" You have taken up my cause, O Lord, you have redeemed my life.

FAITHFULNESS WILL BE REWARDED

ISN'T IT REASSURING that God's steadfast love for us endures forever? This is what we are told in the third chapter of Lamentations, most notably in these verses, where we are reminded that the Lord hears our cries for help no matter how far down in life we may be. If you are at a low point in your life today, this powerful prayer of thanks and praise will empower you to have hope, for there is one who hears you who will help you rise again. That one is God, and he always hears us when we cry out to him.

FAITHFULNESS WILL BE REWARDED

CHAPTER FOUR

PRAYERS

for

GROWTH

A WISH FOR WISDOM
1 Kings 3:6–9 NKJV

You have shown great mercy to your servant David my father, because he walked before you in truth, in righteousness, and in uprightness of heart with you; you have continued this great kindness for him, and you have given him a son to sit on his throne, as it is this day. Now, O Lord my God, you have made your servant king instead of my father David, but I am a little child; I do not know how to go out or come in. And your servant is in the midst of your people whom you have chosen, a great people, too numerous to be numbered or counted. Therefore give to your servant an understanding heart to judge your people, that I may discern between good and evil. For who is able to judge this great people of yours?

ASKING GOD FOR WISDOM

FOR MOST of its history, Israel was a nation in the middle. After their miraculous escape from slavery in Egypt and a 40-year hiatus in the desert, the Israelites settled into their land. But they had to fight for every acre. During this settlement period, a motley collection of regional judges held power.

The prophet Samuel, a judge himself, did much to unite the various tribes, but the people wanted a king. So Samuel selected a tall but brooding warrior named Saul. He was a disaster. In jealousy, he turned the nation's military resources against his best soldier, David. When Saul died in battle against the Philistines, David assumed the throne, restoring order to the monarchy. He built Israel's military presence, neutralizing the Philistines and other foes, and he made plans to build a great temple for the Lord.

When David died, his son Solomon picked up where David had left off, building the Temple and other structures as well as improving the economy. During the reign of Solomon—for one brief, shining period in the 900s B.C.—Israel was the strongest country in the Mideast. Solomon was brilliant at international relations, establishing trade with partners throughout the Mediterranean, Asia, and Africa. Israel was geographically the center of the known world, and it used that position to fill its coffers.

But Solomon also became famous for his wisdom. People came from far and wide to meet him. Where did he get such wisdom? That's where this prayer comes in.

Solomon had been king for a short time when the Lord appeared to him in a dream, offering him anything he wanted. What would you ask for? Wealth? Power? Pleasure? Good looks? Solomon asked for "an understanding heart." Offered anything in the world, he wanted wisdom—and the rest is history.

THE WISDOM OF SOLOMON

SOLOMON ALREADY SHOWED some wisdom in praying his prayer. Here's where we see it.

First, he knew who he was. Yes, he was the son of the great King David, but Solomon didn't assume that made him a worthy successor. He considered himself "a little child." Faced with the huge task of ruling God's people, he felt overwhelmed.

Most of us feel lost when we begin a new job or begin to explore new territory. That's good. We can grow only when we try new things, which are almost always difficult—at least at first. Solomon knew the awesome challenge that lay before him. He knew he needed help, and that's one mark of true wisdom.

Solomon also knew where to find the source of true power. Notice how he used the term "your servant" four times in this prayer. Solomon knew who the real boss was. He acknowledged that those he governed were God's people, not his own. Solomon gave God credit for helping his father, and Solomon believed that he would need even more help.

Ultimately, Solomon knew what had true value. In one variation of an age-old tale, a genie offers a man three wishes. He asks for money and gets it. He asks for power and gets it. Then he asks for more wishes. In a way, Solomon is granted that third wish. Once he had wisdom, there would be no limit to what he could do.

Solomon knew that all the wealth and power he already had would be worthless without the wisdom to use them properly. Implied in his request for wisdom, then, is the idea that Solomon would understand what God wanted. He wanted to "discern between good and evil"—he wanted to know God's way.

In our prayers, we often ask God to agree with our plans when we should be asking for the wisdom to know and do what God would want us to do. Solomon knew the greatest gift he could ask for was the wisdom to know what was right. That's a gift we should seek as well.

TO GIVE FREELY
St. Ignatius

Lord, teach me to be generous.
Teach me to serve you as you deserve;

to give and not to count the cost,
to fight and not to heed the wounds,
to toil and not to seek for rest,
to labor and not to ask for reward,
save that of knowing that I do your will.

GENEROSITY OF SPIRIT

IGNATIUS LOYOLA was a generous and devoted Jesuit priest who served God in innumerable ways. Yet, he still felt the need to ask God how he could be of even greater service, and he never asked for or expected any reward in return. He was willing to put aside his own needs in order to live as God asks.

When we examine our own lives, do we find that our giving comes with a price? Has our work been performed only for what we could gain from it? Did we serve others without asking to be served in return? By looking closely at our own capacity for unconditional love and giving, we may find we are sorely lacking in generosity of spirit.

By focusing on the needs of others and by giving without expecting something in return, we will be doing God's will, and our lives will take on new meaning. Ignatius understood how to truly follow the Lord, and we can, too. Doing God's will for no other reason than to please him is the greatest purpose of all.

BE PATIENT
Catherine Marshall, Adventures in Prayer

Lord Jesus, you know how long I have been praying about this, and I have tried to be patient about an answer. But Lord, why does your providence have to move so slowly?

I know the seasons come and go in majestic sequence. The earth rotates on its axis in a predetermined rhythm. No prayers of mine can change any of this.

But how do I, so earth bound, come to terms with the pace of eternity?

I want to be teachable, Lord. Is there something you want to show me, some block you want removed, some change in me or my attitude before you can answer my prayer? Give me the gift of eyes that see, of ears that hear what you are saying to me.

GOD'S SCHEDULE

GOD ALWAYS answers prayer, but not always with the answer we want. Sometimes it is "Yes." Sometimes it is "No." And sometimes it is "Wait."

"Wait" is the hardest answer of all, but it is one designed right into the universe. Like the farmer who waits for rain, we have to wait for the answer to our prayers. Everything runs on God's schedule, not ours.

It is while we wait that we are transformed. The Spirit of God enriches us with insight and virtue—feeding us with his grace—just as the seed draws nourishment from the deep, dark soil. During this time we learn to trust God and listen to him. We learn what Catherine Marshall here calls "the pace of eternity."

And it all happens while we wait and pray.

THE GIFT OF HARDSHIP
Thomas à Kempis

Lord, make possible for me by grace what is impossible to me by nature. You know that I am not able to endure very much, and that I am downcast by the slightest difficulty.

Grant that for Your sake I may come to love and desire any hardship that puts me to the test, for salvation is brought to my soul when I undergo suffering and trouble for You.

MAKING THE WORLD BETTER

DOWN THROUGH the ages the saints have learned to thank God for their troubles, confident that he will use it to make them—and the world—better. That is what Thomas à Kempis is doing here.

It's not easy to "love and desire" hardship, as this prayer suggests, but it is a mark of maturity to see the significance of hardship and welcome it as an opportunity to trust God and see him at work. Learning to pray this way always draws us closer to the God we love and trust.

MOTHER TERESA'S PRAYER
Mother Teresa

Lord, open our eyes, that we may see you in our brothers and sisters.

Lord open our ears, that we may hear the cries of the hungry, the cold, the frightened, the oppressed.

Lord open our hearts, that we may love each other as you love us.

Renew in us your spirit, Lord.

Free us and make us one.

LEARN FROM THE POOR

FEW PEOPLE have heard the cries of the hungry, the cold, and the frightened the way Mother Teresa did. And none, perhaps, have done so much in response.

Although she had a secure and rewarding ministry as a missionary schoolteacher in India, she decided to leave her convent to live among the poorest of the poor. Her years of sacrificial service did not go unnoticed, and she won the Nobel Peace Prize in 1979 in addition to many other awards and much acclaim.

Nevertheless, her work humbled her. Remembering a time when she had gone out into the streets of Calcutta and brought back a dying woman, Mother Teresa commented that the poor "give us much more than we give them." As Mother Teresa cleaned the woman and put her in bed, the woman clasped Mother Teresa's hand, smiled, and said, "Thank you." Then she died.

This incident moved Mother Teresa deeply. After reflecting on it, she came to the conclusion that if she were dying, she would try to bring attention to herself. "I would have said: 'I am hungry' or 'I am cold' or 'I am dying.'"

Mother Teresa also stressed the fact that pitying the poor keeps us from helping them: "They do not need our sympathy and our pity. They need our love and compassion."

Mother Teresa's request for God to help her to help others changed her life. It can do the same for us.

BONHOEFFER'S LAST PRAYER
Dietrich Bonhoeffer

O God,
Early in the morning I cry unto You.
Help me to pray
And to think only of You.
I cannot pray alone.
In me there is darkness
But with You there is light.
I am lonely but You leave me not.
I am feeble in heart but You leave me not.
I am restless but with You there is peace.
In me there is bitterness, but with You there is patience;
Your ways are past understanding, but
You know the way for me.
You have granted me many blessings:
Now let me accept tribulation from Your hand.

You will not lay on me more than I can bear.
You make all things work together for good
for Your children.

GOD, I TRUST IN YOU

A MAN OF MANY accomplishments, Dietrich Bonhoeffer was a lifelong student of religion and eventually was ordained as a pastor in the German Evangelical Church. He was a highly influential scholar and leader during the 1930s, but his greatest challenge came in the spring of 1943 when, as the leader of the anti-Nazi Confessing Church, he was captured and imprisoned in a Nazi concentration camp for trying to help Jews escape to Switzerland.

Bonhoeffer wrote this prayer for his fellow concentration camp prisoners before being hung at Flossenburg on April 9, 1945. His words live on today as a reminder that no matter where we are in life, God is there, and that no matter how dark things appear to be, God is the light we seek. If a man in Bonhoeffer's terrible position could find a reason to continue to praise and trust God, surely we can, too.

In this powerful prayer of petition, thanksgiving, and surrender, the words speak of a man struggling to overcome the darkness within, as well as the fear, anger, and restlessness that weaken the mind and spirit. And considering his position, who could blame Bonhoeffer for his bitterness? But his prayer tells us that with God we can find the antidote to fear, anger, and restlessness. With God we can find light, peace, comfort, companionship, and patience.

Bonhoeffer must have known the terrible fate that awaited him, for his final verse states he was ready to accept the tribulation from God's hand, knowing that he would not be given more to deal with than he could bear. If we remember this when our own trials challenge us, we can overcome even the greatest obstacles in our path, for truly, as the last line reads, God does make all things work together for the good of his children.

We may not understand how or why God works in the ways he does, but this need not prevent us from having faith in him.

OPENING UP TO GOD
Hugh Prather, The Quiet Answer

I give this time to You alone. Please guide me in this prayer. I ask only for honesty and total sincerity. May I pray from my heart alone. If there is anything I should experience now, or any words I should hear, I am ready to receive them. In stillness and quiet listening, I now open myself to You.

OPEN YOUR WHOLE HEART

WHEN WE OPEN a gift or a letter, we look forward to bringing into view what has been hidden. This is usually a matter of happy anticipation since we hope what others have sent to us will bring us joy.

In the same way, we can open ourselves to God, as Prather's prayer shows us. This surrendering to our Creator will change us if we let it.

Yet, it's not as easy as opening a package, because we may have learned—through painful experience—that when we open ourselves to another, we make ourselves vulnerable and we may not be treated with the kindness and respect that we deserve. This unspoken fear in our hearts may also keep us closed to all that God wants us to experience and hear.

The special, life-changing movement in our lives is this: coming to know our God as so good and gentle and loving that we will have no hesitation to open our hearts to him. Thus, when he invites, we will respond. When he calls, we will listen. When he asks, we will quickly answer. When he knocks, we will open our whole heart.

St. Francis's Devotion
St. Francis of Assisi

May the power of your love, O Lord, fiery and sweet as honey, wean my heart from all that is under heaven, so that I may die for love of your love, you who were so good as to die for love of my love.

A Heart Full of Love

BORN GIOVANNI FRANCESCO di Pietro di Bernardone, the much-beloved St. Francis of Assisi was born into a wealthy family. As a young man, Francis heard God's call to rebuild a local church. Then, in 1209, he sensed a life-long calling to imitate Christ by living a life of chastity, obedience, and poverty.

Francis dramatically abandoned his family wealth and began a life of personal poverty. Once he took his vow, he went to his father and handed him the fancy and expensive clothes off his back. He then borrowed a scarecrow's rope-belt to encircle the ragged robe he would wear for the rest of his life. Though considered a great mystic, he was practical, too; he started a ministry for the sick and directed it until he died.

We can feel the passion of his devotion exuding from this prayer. He asked God to wean his heart from everything on earth that might tempt him to love God any less. If he were with us today, he would invite all of us to do the same.

ROOTED AND GROUNDED
Ephesians 3:16–21

I pray that, according to the riches of his glory, he may grant that you may be strengthened in your inner being with power through his Spirit, and that Christ may dwell in your hearts through faith, as you are being rooted and grounded in love. I pray that you may have the power to comprehend, with all the saints, what is the breadth and length and height and depth, and to know the love of Christ that surpasses knowledge, so that you may be filled with all the fullness of God. Now to him who by the power at work within us is able to accomplish abundantly far more than all we can ask or imagine, to him be glory in the church and in Christ Jesus to all generations, forever and ever. Amen.

INNER STRENGTH

IN THIS PRAYER, Paul lists several things that he's praying for, and the first two go together. He wants his readers to be "strengthened in your inner being," and he wants Christ to "dwell in your hearts." These are two ways of saying the same thing.

If you've been to a gym—or even a park—lately, you've seen people working on improving their outer beings. Many are committed to pumping up, slimming down, and toning their muscles so their bodies have a more attractive outer appearance. Paul wants that sort of attention focused on the inner being.

But who's doing the work here? The Spirit is supplying the power. This seems to be a natural result of Christ taking up residence in our hearts. Perhaps it's like inviting Arnold Schwarzenegger to move into your home; before you know it, he'll have you pumping iron like a champ. Except we're talking about inner fitness, and Christ is our heart-guest. He affects us in deeply personal ways and empowers us with his Spirit.

It's interesting to note that Paul doesn't give us many details about how this strengthening occurs. This is a prayer, after all, not a do-it-yourself manual. The only hint we get is one phrase at the end of verse 17, and it is worded beautifully.

Paul tells us that attaining inner strength involves "being rooted and grounded in love." Rooted is an agricultural term and grounded is architectural. First-century Ephesus was in transition. As with many American cities, there was farmland all around the area, but then a building boom created an urban center, and many people wanted to settle in this center. The citizens knew about the importance of good roots, which draw up nutrients from the soil. They were learning about the importance of a good foundation.

At the end of chapter 2, Paul describes the church as "built upon the foundation of the apostles and prophets, with Christ Jesus himself as the cornerstone. In him the whole structure is joined together and grows into a holy temple to the Lord; in whom you also are built together spiritually into a dwelling place for God" (Ephesians 2:20–22). There, too, Paul mixes metaphors of farming and building. The process of Christian growth combines both of these ideas.

And our foundation is built upon love. It is the starting point of our inner lives. Love is also what we sink our roots into— it continuously nourishes, strengthens, and renews us.

COMPREHEND?

THE NEXT THING Paul prays is that the people would comprehend "what is the breadth and length and height and depth..." Of what? Even in the original Greek, this thought is stopped midsentence. But if you look at the phrases before and after this verse it will be clear that he is talking about love.

When New York City's Empire State Building was constructed, it was the tallest building on earth. People marveled at its size, confused about how there could be a building that tall. That's the image Paul has of God's love. He wants people to put their arms around the hugeness of Christ's love. He wants them not only to "get it" but to grasp it. Yes, it surpasses knowledge, he says, but as Christ moves into their hearts they can make this love a part of their lives.

There was a group known as the Gnostics that became quite prominent in the second century, but we have hints that their ideas were brewing back in Paul's time. Taking some pieces of Christianity, they merged them with parts of Greek philosophy to develop an elaborate system of beliefs. These teachers claimed to have a secret knowledge (*gnosis* in Greek) that few possessed. Others might know little bits and pieces of God, but these privileged "knowers" knew God in his fullness. Or so they said.

We have various groups like that around today, peddling their secret paths to the fullness of God. Paul was clearly launching a barrage against these teachers when he talked about the love of Christ surpassing gnosis. Anyone grounded in this love could experience God's fullness—"secret knowledge" was not required.

ASK AND IMAGINE

PAUL'S BENEDICTION is powerful. You might expect him to assure us that God has the power to give us what we ask for. No, God can do far more than that, more than we could even imagine. What's more, that power is at work within us.

Many philosophies, like that of the Gnostics of old and their modern counterparts, have thrived on making people feel weak and inadequate. Sadly, some Christian teachers have done the same. Sure, we are weak without Christ's power, but that's a moot point once we allow Christ into our hearts. Christ becomes an amazing power working inside of us. If we stay grounded in the incomprehensible love of Christ, the Spirit can do things in us, through us, and around us that are beyond our wildest dreams.

THIRD-STEP PRAYER
From "Alcoholics Anonymous" The Big Book

God, I offer myself to Thee, to build with me and to do with me as Thou wilt. Relieve me of the bondage of self, that I may better do Thy will. Take away my difficulties, that victory over them may bear witness to those I would help of

Thy Power, Thy Love, and Thy Way of life. May I do Thy will always!

BUILD A NEW LIFE

THE 12-STEP PROGRAM of Alcoholics Anonymous has changed millions of lives. People who were lost, alone, forgotten, and diseased have been healed and returned to wholeness by this spiritually empowering program that relies on reaching out to God for help.

This "Third-Step Prayer" is known to all 12-steppers. It requires a total surrender to the will of God—for God to do for us what we could not do for ourselves. So, anyone who is struggling—whether they are struggling with addiction, stress, depression, or anything else—can say this prayer and invite God into their life.

The idea that we can offer ourselves to God to build a new life is truly wonderful and hopeful. To be relieved of the bondage of destructive habits empowers us to live by God's Spirit, through which truth is found. Moreover, to show others our victory over our difficulties is the kind of testimony that can draw them closer to God, too.

Pray this prayer whether you have an addiction or not—whether you are a 12-stepper or not—and you will reap the untold blessings that come from surrendering your life to our heavenly Father.

THE BLESSED PARADOX
Janet Morley, Hymnal: A Worship Book

God our healer, whose mercy is like a refining fire, touch us with your judgment, and confront us with your tenderness; that, being comforted by you, we may reach out to a troubled world, through Jesus Christ.

PRAY FOR THE WORLD

THIS SHORT but penetrating entreaty is a study in paradox: That God's mercy is like a fire—something that can both burn and refine; that we would be "confronted" with tenderness—something usually far removed from confrontation; and that we might use our comfort in order to enter into trouble—something we normally avoid when we feel nurtured and relaxed.

Janet Morley reminds us that all our petitions can be made "through Jesus Christ." When we think of Christ, we see paradox in action.

Christ came to heal and comfort the world, yet he often needed to go away by himself to meditate and pray. He came to save the world, but he had to give his own life in the process.

Similarly, we can approach our lives with the blessed paradox of heaven. If we truly are to make a difference in this troubled world, we'll need to spend much time away from it—in prayer.

It takes courage and faith to turn to you for healing, Lord—to reach out from this darkness to touch the hem of your garment and ask for healing. Please give us the assurance that you will always be with us when we feel weak, frightened, or alone.

ASKING FOR WISDOM
Book of Common Prayer

O God, by whom the meek are guided in judgment, and light rises up in darkness for the godly: Grant us, in all our doubts and uncertainties, to ask what you would have us do; that the spirit of wisdom may save us from all false choices, that in your light we may see light, and in your straight paths we may not stumble, through Jesus Christ our Lord, who lives and reigns with you and the Holy Spirit, one God, for ever and ever.

THE RIGHT CHOICES

JOAN OF ARC is best known for leading soldiers into battle and being burned at the stake for her faith in Christ. There are books, plays, movies, and Web sites about her. Most of the stories about her are true. Although this prayer is associated with her, she probably did not say it.

Whatever legends and myths surrounded her life, one thing is fairly clear; she was a young woman of simple faith who constantly prayed for God to give her wisdom. She deeply felt the responsibility of leadership, and she wanted to make the right choices for those who depended on her.

Most of us will never be recognized as heroic saints; nevertheless, all of us have responsibility for others: our kids, our parents, our co-workers. And we all have battles of our own.

Asking for wisdom, as this prayer does, is something all of us can and should do, for only God's wisdom will steer us on the right course.

BELIEF AND DOUBT
Mark 9:24

Lord, I believe; help my unbelief!

A Desire for Faith

Sometimes, nothing makes sense. We want to believe, but we can't. Even in these times, though, God hears our prayer for help.

A father whose child was troubled by a spirit that sometimes made him mute was the first person we know of to pray this prayer: "Help my unbelief!" It has been prayed countless times since. This man possibly also said to Jesus, "If you can do anything, take pity on us and help us." Jesus saw the boy struggle with the evil spirit and the man struggle with his faith, and he decided to heal them both.

The disciples, who had tried to heal the boy, wanted to know why they couldn't cast the spirit out of him. Jesus said to them, "This kind can come out only through prayer" (v. 29). A prayer for faith is one Jesus is happy to respond to.

God's Perfect Plan
Catherine Marshall, Adventures in Prayer

Father, once—it seems very long ago now—I had such big dreams, so much anticipation of the future. Now no shimmering horizon beckons me.

Where is your plan for my life, Father?

You have told us that without a vision, we perish. So Father in heaven, knowing that I can ask in confidence for what is your expressed will to give me, I ask you to deposit in my mind and heart the particular dream, the special vision you have for my life.

And along with the dream, will you give me whatever graces, patience, and stamina it takes to see the dream through? This may involve adventures I have not bargained for. But I want to trust you enough to follow, even if you lead along new paths.

Lord, if you have to break down any prisons of mine before I can see the stars and catch the vision, then Lord, begin the process now. In joyous expectation. Amen.

FRESH VISION

THE LORD told the prophet Jeremiah, "For surely I know the plans I have for you, plans for your welfare and not for harm, to give you a future with hope. Then when you call upon me and come and pray to me, I will hear you" (Jeremiah 29:11–12). It is evident from these comforting words that our best interests are close to God's heart; prayer can give us hope once we are willing to put our trust in God.

This should be easy to do, but, like Catherine Marshall, we often lose sight of some great promise or vision, discouraged by our present circumstances. In such spiritual despair, we can ask the Lord for a fresh vision and for the strength to achieve that vision.

Wait in "joyous expectation" for God's great blessings to begin in your life.

AN APOSTLE'S PRAYER
Philippians 1:9–11

And this is my prayer, that your love may overflow more and more with knowledge and full insight, to help you determine what is best, so that in the day of Christ you may be pure and blameless, having produced the harvest of righteousness that comes through Jesus Christ for the glory and praise of God.

GROWING IN LOVE AND INSIGHT

PAUL WROTE this letter from prison, either in Rome or Ephesus, yet it is filled with joy. He had been jailed for preaching the message of Christ, but he doesn't bemoan his situation. Instead he finds the good in it—he even spreads the gospel among the soldiers who guard him! It is clear that he cares deeply for the Philippians, who have supported him with prayers and gifts. And so, he begins his letter to the Philippians as he begins most of his letters: He offers thanks to his readers and then prays for them.

Imagine the things he could have prayed. "This is my prayer: that many more people would join the Philippian church…that they would be strong as they face discrimination and persecution for the sake of Christ…that life would go well for the members there, free of illness or tragedy…that I'll be able to get out of jail!" Any of these would be fine things to pray for, but that's not what Paul chose.

There is something basic about this prayer and yet something quite advanced. It's as if the Philippians are entering first grade and receiving their doctorates at the same time. When Jesus was asked to name the greatest commandments in God's law, he mentioned two—love the Lord your God and love your neighbor. Love is square one. Elsewhere, Paul says that without love all the pious acts a person can do are worthless. So it shouldn't surprise us that the apostle prays for the Philippians to have love; it is the most necessary component to living a Christian life. Paul wants to make it clear to his readers that without love we are incapable of following the example Christ set for us.

But what does he pray about this love? That it would over-flow in "knowledge and full insight." Love isn't usually teamed with such qualities, is it? People say that love is blind, and they have a point. Your googly-eyed reaction to that special someone you see across a crowded room—well, that's hardly "knowledge and full insight." But Paul knows that true love doesn't come at first sight; it takes time and commitment. The best picture of love isn't the glazed look of the prom couple, but the people who have been married for 30 years—each one knows all weaknesses of the other—and they are more in love than ever.

Some parents show love to their children by giving them everything they want. Other parents know better. Insightful parents recognize that it is often better to say no. Love does what is best for the child, even if it is difficult and the child doesn't like it.

The Beatles sang, "All you need is love," and who can argue with that? Love is our primary calling. But love without knowledge is weak. People might think they're acting in a loving manner because they try not to hurt anyone or anything. That's a fine beginning, but it's mere puppy love compared to the commitment God wants from us. There are some very loving people who are not grounded enough in knowledge to be able to stand against the pressures of crises and criticisms. They might not be hurting anyone, but they're not actively helping, either.

This is the graduate degree Paul prays for—the grown-up love that understands the situation and still follows Christ's example, treating others with compassion.

LOVE'S SIDE EFFECTS

THE ANCIENT GREEKS loved philosophy. They spent lots of time theorizing about what made something beautiful or excellent or true. The Romans appreciated moral excellence, prizing the personal characteristics that made people great. Philippi had been the home of Alexander the Great, so its culture borrowed heavily from the Greek culture that Alexander loved. But by Paul's time, the city was an outpost of the Roman army, so it also reflected Roman values. Putting these cultures together, you can understand why they'd be interested in determining "what is best."

That's what an insightful love does: It seeks to find the best option in a situation, not the easiest. Love wants the best for everyone involved, and knowledge searches for the best way to make it happen.

Later in his letter, Paul urges his readers to refrain from arguing with one another "so that you may be blameless and innocent…in the midst of a crooked and perverse generation" (2:15). Reputation was especially important in Roman culture, so the Christians in this army town would want to be especially blameless. But we can also guess that slander was beginning to tarnish the Christians in that area. The persecution of Christians wasn't going to happen for another decade or so, but discrimination was certainly going on and Christians probably found themselves falsely blamed for all sorts of things.

But in this prayer Paul is talking about "the day of Christ"—that future time when we stand before the Lord we've been serving. Will he be happy with us? Let your love grow rich with insight, and you will make the best choices, which will ensure that you'll stand "pure and blameless" on that day.

Here's the problem with mixing love and knowledge. The choices you make might not always seem the most loving. Because of your insight, you'll have to engage in "tough love" from time to time. And the choices you make won't always seem like the smartest ones, either. Perhaps you'll take another chance on someone who has failed you because—from past experience—you have faith in them, and you also hope they would do the same for you. People might judge you in any situation, blaming you for being too soft or too hard. No one will really know whether or not you did the right thing until your choices yield results.

Paul prays that your insightful love will lead to good choices that are planted like seeds all around you. You'll stand before God on the last day and say, "All I did was plant some seeds," but he'll point to wagonloads of wonderful things coming over the horizon. Your good choices will have yielded a rich harvest.

TRUSTING GOD
Thomas Merton

My Lord God, I have no idea where I am going. I do not see the road ahead of me. I cannot know for certain where it will end. Nor do I really know myself, and the fact that I think I am following Your will does not mean I am actually doing so. But I believe that the desire to please You does in fact please You.

And I hope I have that desire in all that I am doing. . . . Therefore I will trust You always though I may seem to be lost and in the shadow of death. I will not fear, for You are ever with me, and You will never leave me to face my perils alone.

DESIRE TO PLEASE

WHEN WE don't know what's going on, it's nice to know who we can turn to for help—who's in charge. And it's even more reassuring to know God is on our side.

Regardless of our fears, we can do our best and trust in the Lord to help us.

In this prayer, Thomas Merton, a Trappist monk who helped many others lead a life of contemplation, taps a deeper truth. God still loves us, even when we don't know who we are or what he wants. We can have confidence that our desire to please God pleases God.

For Merton, desire is the thing we offer. If we desire God in everything, he will find us even when we feel lost.

In fact, he never lost track of us. And he never will.

THE SHIP OF LIFE
Basil of Caesarea

Steer the ship of my life, good Lord, to your quiet harbor, where I can be safe from the storms of sin and conflict. Show me the course I should take. Renew in me the gift of discernment, so that I can always see the right direction in which I should go. And give me the strength and the courage to choose the right course, even when the sea is rough and the waves are high, knowing that through enduring hardship and danger in your name we shall find comfort and peace.

LET GOD LEAD

BASIL OF CAESAREA (c. 330–379) did indeed let the Lord steer his ship, giving up a career in public life to become a monk in Eastern Asia Minor. He built schools and hospitals, and he also cared for the poor—particularly lepers and other outcasts of society. In one of many prayers composed by this deeply religious man, Basil compares life to a ship and asks the Lord to plot his course.

When we ask God to take over the ship of our own lives, we know not only that we will be led in the right direction but also that we will be protected through the roughest of times. God's intention is to lead us to a peaceful shore, where our destiny awaits—if we are willing to give up control and let God be the wind that fills our sails.

IN GOD'S SIGHT
Book of Common Prayer

Heavenly Father, in you we live and move and have our being: We humbly pray you will guide and govern us by your Holy Spirit, that in all the cares and occupations of our life we may not forget you, but may remember that we are ever walking in your sight; through Jesus Christ our Lord. Amen.

SMILING HEAVENLY EYES

WHAT DOES IT MEAN to "remember" that we are ever in God's sight? For this day, let it be a gentle reminder that smiling heavenly eyes rest upon your shoulders, no matter where you are, no matter the problems you face.

God's loving Spirit is always with us, ready to take our hands and lead us through this life to the eternal life in the Lord's heavenly kingdom.

HERE I AM
Brother Lawrence

My God,
here I am,
my heart devoted to you.
Fashion me
according to your heart.

CENTERED ON GOD

HIS BIRTH NAME was Nicolas Herman, but he became known to history as Brother Lawrence, a monk who lived in the 17th century. We might think of him as a religious chef, for he spent much of his time in the kitchen, either cooking or scrubbing pots and pans. His set of spiritual maxims have urged believers in Christ to "practice the presence of God," no matter where they may be.

The beauty of this direct approach to God is that it makes the divine-human relationship quite real and available. Even if we are washing the dishes or mowing the lawn, our hearts can be centered on God.

THE PEACE PRAYER OF ST. FRANCIS
St. Francis of Assisi

Lord, make me an instrument of Your peace:
where there is hatred, let me show love;
where there is injury, pardon;
where there is doubt, faith;
where there is despair, hope;
where there is darkness, light;
and where there is sadness, joy.
O Divine Master, grant that I may not so much seek
to be consoled as to console,
to be understood as to understand,
to be loved as to love.

For it is in giving that we receive,
it is in pardoning that we are pardoned,
and it is in dying that we are born to eternal life.

PEACE IN YOUR HEART

THE "PEACE PRAYER of St. Francis" is one of the most famous and repeated prayers in the world. In praying that he be a vessel through which God's love might touch others, Francis prayed a classic prayer for the spiritual welfare of others.

Francis of Assisi (1182–1226) dedicated his life to serving the sick and poverty-stricken in the world. Not many of us take Jesus' words about forsaking all earthly possessions literally, but Francis did. For example, as a young man, Francis was once hauled before the local bishop. It seems his father had demanded that Francis return all that he owed him. In response, Francis stripped himself naked and sent home the clothes off his back! He then took beggar's clothes and subsequently spent many years ministering among lepers.

Despite the fact that many people associate this prayer with St. Francis, the authorship of the prayer is actually uncertain. Some scholars date it from the early part of the 20th century. They point to the fact that it was found in Normandy in 1915, written on the back of a holy card of St.

Francis, from which the name comes. Other historians ascribe it to a time before St. Francis, and some believe he did indeed write it.

In any case, all agree that the words of this prayer are an eloquent statement for peace and they reflect the philosophy of St. Francis. To give back only good for evil, to always retreat in the face of brutality, to offer peace and love in the face of cruelty—these are the values, which, if each individual took them to heart, would transform the world. On our war-torn earth, made even more dangerous by global terrorism, what finer prayer could there be to utter than this one?

Despite Francis' remarkable compassion for others, some viewed Francis as somewhat odd. For example, he even preached to the animals! Yet, one commentator said of him, "Since the nineteenth century, Roman Catholics and Protestants have increasingly seen spiritual sanity in his worldly irrationality....Francis is frequently referred to as either the peculiar saint among the rosebushes or as the conscience of Western civilization, or both."

There is no doubt that Francis can speak to our consciences today. Will we listen? "While you are proclaiming peace with your lips," said Francis, "be careful to have it even more fully in your heart."

CHAPTER FIVE

PRAYERS
of
THANKS
and PRAISE

AMAZING GRACE
John Newton

Amazing Grace! How sweet the sound,
That saved a wretch like me!
I once was lost, but now am found,
Was blind, but now I see.
'Twas grace that taught my heart to fear,
and grace my fears relieved.
How precious did that grace appear
The hour I first believed.
Thro' many dangers, toils and snares,
I have already come;
'Tis grace hath bro't me safe thus far,
and grace will lead me home.
When we've been there ten thousand years,
Bright shining as the sun,
We've no less days to sing God's praise
Than when we first begun.

A SPIRITUAL JOURNEY

IF ANYONE could have proclaimed the power of God's merciful grace, it was John Newton. At age 7, he lost his mother, and by age 11, he hit the high seas with his father. Soon he became a man of reckless abandon and godless sin serving on ships that enslaved people in Africa and sold them to slave traders. Eventually Newton became captain of his own slave ship, but his wicked life would be challenged when he encountered a violent storm at sea that would change his life and inspire him to write this classic hymn.

During that storm, Newton read Thomas à Kempis' book, *Imitation of Christ*, and the book's message, combined with the frightening storm, served as the basis for Newton's eventual acceptance of Christ as his Savior. Thus began a spiritual journey that over the years would transform him from a wretched sinner to a crusader for Christ's teachings. At the age of 39, he was ordained an Anglican minister. He died at age 82, a man of great faith and gratitude for God's grace, which he believed had saved his soul.

"Amazing Grace" has gone on to become one of the greatest, most repeated hymns of all time, sung across the world in churches and centers of worship and at funerals and military memorials. Musicians have performed it in every style. But to those of us who feel a personal call to this prayerful hymn, the words describe our own quiet and reverent awe of a God who could save even the most lowly and sinful and restore spiritual vision to those blinded by fear.

That something as mysterious as grace exists for all of us, no matter how poor or lost or distraught, gave Newton reason to sing out in praise of God. He wanted to thank God for watching over him even in his darkest and most troubled moments, times he described as "many dangers, toils and snares." Even now, millions of people the world over have experienced that very grace in their own lives. They have felt their hearts soar in joyful praise for the goodness of a God who never deserts us.

Whether we whisper, speak, shout, or sing "Amazing Grace" matters not, for the words harbor such transforming power and humility in any form, especially when we are at a point in our lives when we are ready and willing to give ourselves to God. That is what makes this prayer so profound: It speaks of despair, hope, renewal, and salvation.

That a wretch could be saved, that those of us who feel lost and alone and afraid could be led home again, that we are safe in God's eternal love no matter how we've sinned or what mistakes we've made, these are the messages of "Amazing Grace." How sweet it is!

GOD IS EVERYWHERE
Psalm 139:7–10, 14–18

Where can I go from your spirit? Or where can I flee from your presence? If I ascend to heaven, you are there; if I make my bed in Sheol, you are there. If I take the wings of the morning and settle at the farthest limits of the sea, even there your hand shall lead me, and your right hand shall hold me fast.

I praise you, for I am fearfully and wonderfully made. Wonderful are your works; that I know very well. My frame was not hidden from you, when I was being made in secret, intricately woven in the depths of the earth. Your eyes beheld my unformed substance. In your book were written all the days that were formed for me, when none of them as yet existed. How weighty to me are your thoughts, O God! How vast is the sum of them! I try to count them—they are more than the sand; I come to the end—I am still with you.

A GOOD PLAN

GOD IS EVERYWHERE. This thought can be either comforting or terrifying. If God is everywhere, he sees us not only when we want him to see us but also when we don't want him to see us. Although the psalmist knew this about God, he found comfort in this truth. Whether we are far out at sea or deep within the womb, God is still with us, leading us and holding us fast.

The writer finds this comforting because he was "wonderfully made" (v. 14). In fact, God had a plan for his entire life: "In your book were written all the days that were formed for me, when none of them as yet existed" (v. 16).

This is a life-changing thought. God knows our end before our beginning. He has a plan for us, and we can have faith that it is a good plan because God himself is good.

CLOTHED IN LIGHT
Psalm 104:1–4

Bless the Lord, O my soul. O Lord my God, you are very great. You are clothed with honor and majesty, wrapped in light as with a garment. You stretch out the heavens like a tent, you set the beams of your chambers on the waters, you make the clouds your chariot, you ride on the wings of the wind, you make the winds your messengers, fire and flame your ministers.

PURE, TRUE, AND LOVELY

OUR GOD is a big God. He rides the clouds and sets the foundation of his dwelling on the sea. Even more remarkable are his clothes. The Lord is clothed in majesty and light. Majesty is more difficult to comprehend, so it is often the "light" that we focus on. We know what light looks like and we know what it does.

Light helps us see the path we should take. More importantly, it dispels the darkness, helping us see danger, as well as opportunity. This is good because we are often blinded to that which is pure, true, and lovely.

Praise God that his light extends everywhere. Fire and flame are his ministers, and his light both helps us see and keeps us warm.

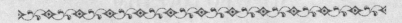

BLESS YOU AND KEEP YOU
Numbers 6:24–26

The Lord bless you and keep you;
the Lord make his face to shine upon you,
and be gracious to you;
the Lord lift up his countenance upon you,
and give you peace.

PRAYER FOR GOOD GRACES

THE LORD GAVE this prayerlike benediction through Moses to Aaron and his sons as a way to greet the ancient Israelites. It was the Lord's way of blessing and showing his delight in his people.

Throughout history, this prayer has been exchanged as a blessing between friends and strangers alike. It is a way to acknowledge one another and wish one another the good graces that the Lord can bestow upon his beloved children.

ALL WHO LOVE HIM
Psalm 145:13–21

For your kingdom is an everlasting kingdom. You rule generation after generation.

The Lord is faithful in all he says; he is gracious in all he does. The Lord helps the fallen and lifts up those bent beneath their loads. All eyes look to you for help; you give them their food as they need it. When you open your hand, you satisfy the hunger and thirst of every living thing. The Lord is righteous in everything he does; he is filled with kindness. The Lord is close to all who call on him, yes, to all who call on him sincerely. He fulfills the desires of those who fear him; he hears their cries for help and rescues them. The Lord protects all those who love him, but he destroys the wicked.

I will praise the Lord, and everyone on earth will bless his holy name forever and forever.

God Satisfies Our Needs

THIS PSALM is about a great God filled with promises for all in need. He is close to all who call on him; he helps the fallen; he lifts up those bent beneath their loads; and he protects all those who love him.

The psalmist reminds us of the faithfulness of God's words and the graciousness of his deeds, the most amazing of which is "satisfying the hunger and thirst of every living thing." He gives us, as the apostle Paul put it, "more than we can ask or imagine" (Ephesians 3:20).

Victory Song
Exodus 15:1–18

Then Moses and the Israelites sang this song to the Lord: "I will sing to the Lord, for he has triumphed gloriously; horse and rider he has thrown into the sea. The Lord is my strength and my might, and he has become my salvation, this is my God, and I will praise him, my father's God, and I will exalt him. The Lord is a warrior; the Lord is his name.

"Pharaoh's chariots and his army he cast into the sea; his picked officers were sunk in the Red Sea. The floods cov-

ered them; they went down into the depths like a stone. Your right hand, O Lord, glorious in power—your right hand, O Lord, shattered the enemy. In the greatness of your majesty you overthrew your adversaries; you sent out your fury, it consumed them like stubble. At the blast of your nostrils the waters piled up, the floods stood up in a heap; the deeps congealed in the heart of the sea. The enemy said, 'I will overtake, I will divide the spoil, my desire shall have its fill of them. I will draw my sword, my hand shall destroy them.' You blew with your wind, the sea covered them; they sank like lead in the mighty waters.

"Who is like you, O Lord, among the gods? Who is like you, majestic in holiness, awesome in splendor, doing wonders? You stretched out your right hand, the earth swallowed them.

"In your steadfast love you led the people whom you redeemed; you guided them by your strength to your holy abode. The peoples heard, they trembled; pangs seized the inhabitants of Philistia. Then the chiefs of Edom were dismayed; trembling seized the leaders of Moab; all the inhabitants of Canaan melted away. Terror and dread fell upon them; by the might of your arm they became still as a stone until your people, O Lord, passed by, until the people whom you acquired passed by. You brought them in and planted them on the mountain of your own possession, the place, O Lord, that you made your abode, the sanctuary, O Lord, that your hands have established. The Lord will reign forever and ever."

GOD'S MIRACULOUS WORKS

HOLLYWOOD HAS perfected the chase scene. According to the formula of most action films, we see the fleeing heroes and the chasers gaining on them. Then the camera cuts back and forth until the heroes find themselves up against an insurmountable obstacle—for instance, a train crossing the road in front of them. They'll be caught for sure! But then they find some miraculous way over that obstacle—maybe using a dump truck to vault over the train. The heroes are safe!

Did you know that formula was borrowed from the book of Exodus? More than 3,000 years ago, the Israelites found themselves in a similar chase scene. Moses had brought God's demands to the Pharaoh of Egypt: "Let my people go!" Pharaoh resisted until a series of plagues weakened his nation. Eventually, he released the Israelites from slavery and sent them on their way toward Canaan.

So we see a million or more Israelites beginning their journey out of Egypt. Meanwhile, Pharaoh has second thoughts: "What have we done?" (Exodus 14:5). He sends his cavalry after the fleeing former slaves. Moses and the Israelite traveling party have reached the banks of the Red Sea; they can't go any farther. Word comes from the rear guard that Egyptian troops are gaining ground. The people complain, "So you set us free just to die out here? Aren't there enough graves in Egypt?"

But Moses turns to the Lord, who tells him to stretch his arms out over the sea. Miraculously, it parts, leaving a pathway for the Israelites to tread. God has sent a dark cloud to confuse the advancing Egyptians; they're in a panic. When all the Israelites have crossed, Moses extends his arms and the sea returns to its normal depth, drowning the Egyptians who had just begun to cross. The Israelites move on safely toward the Promised Land.

As you might expect, this wondrous miracle sparked a great celebration. Moses led the people in a song of praise for God's deliverance. Miriam gathered the women. "I will sing to the Lord, for he has triumphed gloriously" (Exodus 15:1, 21) they sang.

The crossing of the Red Sea became the defining moment for the Lord's people. Previously, they were just a band of slaves; now they were a nation. They once seemed to have little awareness of their God; now he had proved himself. The Scriptures often refer to this miracle as a moment when the Lord showed his great power to save.

LIKE NO OTHER

MOST PEOPLE in the ancient world believed in multiple gods. The Egyptians had many gods, each specializing in a specific area of life; so did the Canaanites and Babylonians. Some gods were associated with nations. This was how others viewed the God of Israel. No one denied that he existed; they just put him in a group with the other deities. When one nation defeated another in battle, it was seen as proof that their gods were greater than the gods of the losers.

We find this "battle of the gods" idea often in Scripture. Of course, the Lord is eager to show that he is the one and only God. But at times he is also exalted as being better than all the others. That's what we find in this victory song.

"Who is like you?" the people ask. The answer is, of course, no one. Majestic and awesome, the Lord God of Israel is far superior to any other nation's deity.

The verb tenses in the last paragraph of the song make it seem as if this was written after the Israelites had settled in Canaan. Some scholars think that an editor might have added extra verses to the song some time later. But it also sounds like the wishful thinking of a team that has scored a big victory in its first game. All those nations lay between Egypt and a successful settlement of the Promised Land. God would have to establish dominance over all of them, and after this first mighty miracle, was there any question about what he could do?

Yet it really wasn't as easy as these verses make it sound. Because they feared the Canaanites, Israel wandered for 40 years in the desert. Edom and Moab were fairly easy foes to vanquish once the Israelites finally got there, but the Canaanites proved pesky, and the Philistines remained tough for a few centuries. So if this section is a later edition, it glosses over the tough realities. If it's planning ahead, we can forgive a bit of over-confidence.

But this victory song isn't just a historical relic. It is full of some very rich words that affect our lives as much as they affected the Israelites. "Steadfast love" translates the Hebrew word *hesed* about as well as any English phrase can. It is love that goes over and above what's expected, a love that lasts forever. It is God's kind of love. Redeeming is a buying back. It's very appropriate in this context, because redeeming is something done for slaves whose freedom is purchased. This victory song is clearly talking about God bringing people out of slavery and leading them to the Promised Land. But the verse can also refer to God's dealings with any of us in any period of history. We can become enslaved in many ways—to possessions, passions, or addictions. In his steadfast love, our God can set us free.

MAGNIFICAT
Luke 1:46–55 NLT

Mary responded, "Oh, how I praise the Lord. How I rejoice in God my Savior! For he took notice of his lowly servant girl, and now generation after generation will call me blessed. For he, the Mighty One, is holy, and he has done great things for me. His mercy goes on from generation to generation, to all who fear him. His mighty arm does tremendous things! How he scatters the proud and haughty ones! He has taken princes from their thrones and exalted the lowly. He has satisfied the hungry with good things and sent the rich away with empty hands. And how he has helped his servant Israel! He has not forgotten his promise to be merciful. For he promised our ancestors—Abraham and his children—to be merciful to them forever.

GOD'S GREAT POWER

SHE WAS just a teenager, promised in marriage to a carpenter named Joseph. One day the angel Gabriel appeared to her and announced that she would bear a special child. Her son would reign over an eternal kingdom, taking the throne of David to new levels. He would be the Son of the Most High God.

Mary was stunned. First of all, she was a virgin. But the angel explained that such a miraculous birth would be possible for God. Mary responded in agreeable trust. "Here am I, the servant of the Lord; let it be with me according to your word" (Luke 1:38).

Shortly afterward, she visited with her cousin Elizabeth, who was carrying a miraculous child of her own, the child who would be known as John the Baptist. Elizabeth was full of praise for Mary, but Mary was quick to deflect it toward God. The song she sang at that point has been dubbed "The Magnificat" (from the Latin). It's a unique prayer of praise for God's actions in history, culminating in his gift of the Christ-child to a poor Jewish girl.

MARY'S MAGNIFYING GLASS

MARY BEGINS HER SONG by magnifying the Lord. One meaning of that word is to glorify or exalt, but there's more. To magnify is also to make something bigger, just as you might study a map with a magnifying glass. Mary sings about the greatness of God and hopes his reputation will grow even greater.

In turn, the rest of the song deals with how God "magnifies" his people. In the first few verses, Mary sings about her own situation. God has chosen a lowly servant girl from Galilee and has done great things for her. As a result, she says, "all generations will call me blessed"—a prophecy that is still being fulfilled today. But she is not bragging. Mary knows she's a nobody who has been selected for a special honor.

The next section of the Magnificat expands the focus. Not only has God done this amazing thing for Mary, but he does this sort of thing all the time. He lifts the lowly and topples the mighty. When people show pride, he humbles them. When people humbly honor him, he exalts them.

This theme parallels much of Jesus' preaching in later years. He told his disciples, for instance, to avoid taking the seat of honor at a banquet. Better to be bumped up to a nicer seat than demoted. "For all who exalt themselves will be humbled, and those who humble themselves will be exalted" (Luke 14:11).

The kingdom of God, Jesus often preached, would look like an upside-down place to most people. The people who thought they had it made realize they don't. Prostitutes and tax collectors will get to God's kingdom before the religious leaders. Why? Because they were humble enough to realize they needed the grace God offered.

It's interesting to see that Mary, with Jesus still in her womb, was already in tune with him. God knew it would be this way; this is, perhaps, why God chose Mary. We can only wonder how much Jesus' ideas were shaped by Mary as he grew up.

In the final verses of this prayer, Mary focuses on the nation of Israel. Her child was the Messiah, the promised deliverer. She could have chosen any number of messianic prophecies from the Hebrew Scriptures, but she went back to the beginning of the Jewish nation. On several occasions, God had spoken to Abraham, promising that Abraham would become the father of a great nation.

That promise had come true; the nation of Israel had developed and flourished. But God also told Abraham, "All the families of the earth will be blessed through you" (Genesis 12:3).

This is, no doubt, the prophecy Mary has in mind. She knew the Messiah's kingdom would break through national boundaries. It would include Jews and people of all nations. As the elderly watchman Simeon prayed eight days after Jesus' birth, this child would become "a light for revelation to the Gentiles and for glory to your people Israel" (Luke 2:32).

You might expect a young woman to be in shock over the news of a virgin birth. You might expect Mary to focus on her own needs at such a time. But in this prayer she sees the big picture. She turns her magnifying glass on these events and sees that this isn't just a young woman's miraculous pregnancy in an obscure village near Galilee. God is doing that topsy-turvy thing he always does, and he is lighting a torch in Israel that will enlighten the whole world.

Mary was certainly an extraordinary woman, but it's because of what God enabled her to do. Her message is that God uses ordinary folks to do extraordinary things. Princes are toppled, and common people like Mary are raised up for God's work. Feel incapable of doing what God wants? Join the club. But it's God's power, not yours, that will accomplish great things through you.

A Soldier's Prayer
Author Unknown

I asked God for strength, that I might achieve.
I was made weak, that I might learn humbly to obey.
I asked for health, that I might do greater things.
I was given infirmity, that I might do better things.
I asked for riches, that I might be happy.
I was given poverty, that I might be wise.
I asked for power, that I might have the praise of men.
I was given weakness, that I might feel the need of God.
I asked for all things, that I might enjoy life.
I was given life, that I might enjoy all things.
I got nothing that I asked for—but everything that I had hoped for.
Almost despite myself, my unspoiled prayers were answered.
I am among all men, most richly blessed.

LIFE IS JOY

THIS PRAYER is believed to have been part of a letter found on the body of a Confederate soldier killed in the line of duty. We may never know his true identity, but his profound words live on in this powerful prayer about the grace of God's will.

This soldier prayed for many things. He asked for strength, health, riches, power—all the typical things a man desires. Instead, God gave him greater blessings by giving him the opposite of what he desired. God chose to give the soldier weakness, infirmity, and poverty, and the end result was that all the desires of the soldier's heart were answered in a way he never could have imagined. He, indeed, received nothing he asked for, but everything he had hoped for.

This prayer joyfully proves that God knows best what we need and that his vision for us always outshines our own limited vision for ourselves. The author may not have been healthy, rich, or powerful, as he had hoped, but he was made wise, humble, and prosperous in the important things worth having—the joys of life itself. He learned what Jesus taught his disciples—to seek God's kingdom first and all else will be given to you as a result.

Have you ever prayed for something, only to later feel relieved that God did not answer your prayer? That, in fact, God had brought you something greater than what your mind could have conceived? This is what A Soldier's Prayer is about: God truly knows what we want and need, even when we are not sure of it ourselves.

The lesson the soldier learned was that he was given the supreme gift—life—which allowed him to "enjoy all things." In the end, this was what he was able to learn, what his life taught him—what a treasure life is.

"Almost despite myself," the soldier writes, "my unspoiled prayers were answered." We can remember this the next time our prayers are not answered or are answered in a way that makes us question God's intentions. Perhaps, almost despite ourselves, when we pray from our hearts, we will get not what we wanted but what we were destined to have.

POWER WITHIN US
Ephesians 3:20–21

Now to him who by the power at work within us is able to accomplish abundantly far more than we can ask or imagine, to him be glory in the church and in Christ Jesus to all generations, forever and ever. Amen.

WELCOME GOD'S POWER

THE APOSTLE PAUL knew it was God's power within each of us that makes us successful. He also knew the glory should always go to God.

In Paul's letter to the Ephesians, he created a prayer of gratitude that resonates in our hearts with the truth that we are vessels for God's love. When we come to know that it is not by our own hands that we achieve but by the hands of God guiding us, we realize just how miraculous life can be.

Have you ever struggled to do something, only to find that no matter how hard you worked, it would not "click"? Perhaps you were not allowing God's power to work in your life. For God does not work for us but through us.

PERFECT IN WEAKNESS
2 Corinthians 12:8–9

Three times I appealed to the Lord about this, that it would leave me, but he said to me, "My grace is sufficient for you, for power is made perfect in weakness." So, I will boast all the more gladly of my weaknesses, so that the power of Christ may dwell in me.

THE BEAUTY OF IMPERFECTION

PAUL OF TARSUS, the author of this letter to the Corinthian church, was known as the "apostle to the Gentiles." He established churches throughout the Mediterranean world whose members were mostly Gentiles. Paul preached the message of God's goodness to anyone who would listen.

Paul was no stranger to the marvelous workings of God's grace in his own life. Some biblical historians believe that Paul suffered from a distressing malady such as epilepsy or perhaps blindness.

Whatever Paul's weakness was, he affirms something in this cry for mercy that we can all take to heart: If, after asking for relief, it does not seem to come, we can assume God's glory is better served by a display of his power *in the midst of* our weaknesses.

Perhaps the Lord is using us to teach other people, or perhaps he is trying to teach us something. Whatever the reason, Paul knew that to be used by the Lord is a great blessing.

THE CENTER OF FAITH
Psalm 118:1–9

Give thanks to the Lord, for he is good! His faithful love endures forever.

*Let the congregation of Israel repeat: "His faithful love
endures forever." Let Aaron's descendants, the priests,
repeat: "His faithful love endures forever." Let all who fear
the Lord repeat: "His faithful love endures forever."*

*In my distress I prayed to the Lord; and the Lord answered
and rescued me. The Lord is for me, so I will not be afraid.
What can mere mortals do to me? Yes, the Lord is for me;
he will help me. I will look in triumph at those who hate
me. It is better to trust the Lord than to put confidence in
people. It is better to trust the Lord than to put confidence
in princes.*

THE GREATEST COMMANDMENT

THIS IS an interesting text, perhaps made more interesting
by the fact that it is exactly in the center of the Bible. If
you count the verses in front of it and the verses behind it,
you will find that at the exact numerical center of the
Scriptures it says this: "It is better to trust the Lord than to
put confidence in people" (v. 8).

This is also the exact center of what the Scriptures teach
us: That we must put our faith in God instead of people. He
is the Creator and our heavenly Father. Jesus said the first
and greatest commandment was that we should love the
Father with all of our heart. Everything the Bible teaches
begins and ends with this commandment.

Obviously the way we love God is by trusting him, especially in view of how this particular prayer begins. We are told four times that "his faithful love endures forever." And then we are told, twice, that he is for us.

Martin Luther related this truth in a hymn: "A mighty fortress is our God, a bulwark never changing." And it is a truth that caused the ancient Hebrew king who wrote this prayer to also say, "Some take pride in chariots, and some in horses, but our pride is in the name of the Lord our God" (Ps. 20:7). The missionary pioneer Hudson Taylor knew it, too, and on his death bed, he said, "I can only lie still in God's arms like a little child, and trust him."

A faithful God with faithful love. What's not to trust? No wonder it is better to take refuge in the Lord than to put our confidence in other people. It is a truth that rightly belongs at the center of our faith and our lives.

HOW MAJESTIC!
Psalm 8 NLT

O Lord, our Lord, the majesty of your name fills the earth!
Your glory is higher than the heavens. You have taught
children and nursing infants to give you praise. They

silence your enemies who were seeking revenge. When I look at the night sky and see the work of your fingers—the moon and the stars you have set in place—what are mortals that you should think of us, mere humans that you should care for us? For you made us only a little lower than God, and you crowned us with glory and honor. You put us in charge of everything you made, giving us authority over all things—the sheep and the cattle and all the wild animals, the birds in the sky, the fish in the sea, and everything that swims the ocean currents. O Lord, our Lord, the majesty of your name fills the earth!

MARVELING AT GOD'S CREATION

SOMETIMES the beauty of nature takes your breath away. Maybe it's a sunset that paints colors you've never seen before across the entire sky. Maybe it's the horizon across a tranquil lake on a sunny summer afternoon, or mountains so high and majestic they reach into the clouds. It could be a dappled butterfly dancing on air above a beautiful rose in bloom, or a glistening horse in full gallop, or the inky expanse of the night sky flecked with bright stars. Scientists have explanations for each of these; they can tell you why we see colors at dusk, and how a butterfly stays aloft. And they have plenty of theories about that starry night sky. But in those breathless moments, we recognize something that goes beyond all science: There is a Creator, and he is awesome.

The psalmist finds himself in such a moment as he prays the prayer of Psalm 8. The writing is credited to David, and we might imagine him in his youth, tending sheep on a Bethlehem hillside, gazing up at the moon and stars, and wondering about the God who put them there.

Yet the main point of this psalm is not the glory of creation but the amazing status of human beings. See how the song unfolds. It first asks the breathtaking question: In view of all the glories God has made, who are we? How can you, God, possibly care about us when you've got all those stars to light up? We do seem awfully insignificant.

We can surely relate to that mind-set, but the psalm turns a corner, answering the question in a surprising way. Somehow, God doesn't consider us insignificant at all. He has crowned us with glory and honor, giving us a place of honor second only to himself. The beautiful things we marvel at are under our dominion. (This is clearly a reference to Genesis 1:28, where the first humans are given charge over the earth.)

In the movie *Big,* a boy gets his wish to be "bigger" and instantly becomes an adult. He lands a job as an executive in a toy company. Throughout the film, we see the business world through this youngster's eyes. He often has an attitude of "I can't believe I'm actually in charge of stuff!" That's somewhat the attitude we find in Psalm 8. "We're a bunch of nobodies, but look at what God has done for us!"

God keeps surprising us. He creates a magnificent world that makes us feel small, but then he puts us in charge of it.

Jesus once said that God has counted every hair on our heads. Surely he has better things to do than that! But no, that's how much he cares for us. What are human beings? Fallible, yes. Sinful, yes. Disappointing, often. But still we are surprisingly loved by our awesome Creator, who has endless faith in us.

GREAT IS HIS FAITHFULNESS
Lamentations 3:22–24 NLT

The unfailing love of the Lord never ends! By his mercies we have been kept from complete destruction. Great is his faithfulness; his mercies begin afresh each day. I say to myself, "The Lord is my inheritance; therefore, I will hope in him!"

GOD'S LOVE AMONG THE RUINS

YOU WOULDN'T EXPECT to find such a strong note of hope in a book called Lamentations. The prophet Jeremiah had plenty to lament about. The city of Jerusalem had been overrun by the Babylonian army. Many people had been carted off to captivity. The Temple had been torn down and its treasures looted. As he began this book, the prophet pictured Jerusalem as a lonely widow, weeping all night.

What made it worse for Jeremiah was that he knew exactly why this had happened. The people had turned away from the Lord. Jeremiah himself had delivered God's message of doom again and again, but the people had just laughed it off. God would never let his own Temple be destroyed, would he?

Yes, he would. He did. And Jeremiah saw it coming.

The prophet escaped to Egypt during the Babylonian onslaught, but sometime later he wandered back to the holy city, poking through the ruins. "Look and see if there is any sorrow like my sorrow" (Lamentations 1:12), he wrote.

Halfway through this book of mourning, however, Jeremiah remembered something. Moments after saying, "I have forgotten what happiness is" (Lamentations 3:17), he added, "But this I call to mind, and therefore I have hope." That leads us into this prayer.

Mourning to Morning

It doesn't start like a prayer, but rather Jeremiah offers new insight about the Lord's love: "By his mercies we have been kept from complete destruction." It's easy to imagine the prophet sifting through the ashes and forgetting about God. In fact, in the earlier chapters he mentioned that there was no one around to offer comfort. But then this ray of hope peeks through, like the first hint of dawn. I am still alive, and God is still here with me!

You can almost hear the gears shifting in the prophet's brain. God has judged us, but he never stopped loving us. He promised destruction if the people refused to repent, and that did happen, but he's been loving us all the way through. This tragedy isn't a failure of God's love; it's a failure of our ability to obey him. His love is steadfast. His faithfulness is great. If we turn back to him now in our misery, he will help us put things back together!

God's mercies begin afresh each day. Every day he's looking for a different way to show his tender love for us. For Jeremiah, this newness was especially important. He and his city needed a new start. One of the first big "disaster movies," *The Poseidon Adventure*, had a hit song—"The Morning After"—that played at the end. That's where Jeremiah was. The disaster had struck; now he needed a "morning after" in which his loving Lord would show him the way.

"The Lord is my portion," says Jeremiah. That's an interesting word that means just what you think it does. Mom carves up the casserole, and Sally gets this portion, and

Billy gets this portion, and Jeremiah gets…the Lord. At the reading of the will, the wife gets the mansion and the cars, the son gets the trust fund, and Jeremiah gets…the Lord. The whole point is: The Lord is enough for him. The city had nothing left, but if the people accepted the portion that they still had—the Lord—they could renew their hope and get on with their lives.

The same is true for us. Disasters happen in our lives. It's tempting to spend a lot of time evaluating why they happened. Did we bring it on ourselves, or did someone else mess up? And why would God allow suffering, anyway? Jeremiah doesn't invite us into that debate. He just points to the dawning of God's new mercies. This is our portion, the steadfast love of God, and that is enough for us. So pick up a brick—it's time to start building anew.

God's Glories
Romans 11:33–36

O the depth of the riches and wisdom and knowledge of God! How unsearchable are his judgments and how inscrutable his ways! "For who has known the mind of the Lord? Or who has been his counselor? Or who has given a gift to him, to receive a gift in return?" For from him and through him and to him are all things. To him be the glory forever. Amen.

PRICELESS BLESSINGS

IN PAUL'S LETTER to Rome, he praised the depths of God's glories in hope that his fellow Christians in Rome would understand that the Lord is all-knowing, all-powerful, and all-giving. Paul compels us not to question the judgments and ways of the Lord, for we cannot know his mind.

When we pray to God in faith, trusting that his ways are best, our prayers are always heard and answered. Remember Paul's words: "from him and through him and to him are all things." God knows our hearts—our innermost desires—and he gives priceless blessings accordingly.

When we glorify God in prayer, we invite his miracles into our lives.

EXTOL OUR LORD!
Psalm 145:1–4

I will extol you, my God and King, and bless your name forever and ever. Every day I will bless you, and praise your name forever and ever. Great is the Lord, and greatly to be praised; his greatness is unsearchable. One generation shall laud your works to another, and shall declare your mighty acts.

LOOK UP

THE PSALMIST invites us to live in light of God's goodness. To extol him is to tell him: You are an awesome God. Having an attitude of praise has tremendous life-changing potential. The challenge is simply to look up more than we look down. It's easy to become focused on all of life's disappointments. Yet, when we take a moment and become aware of God's presence, our perspective radically changes. For example, when we appreciate the warmth of the sun shining down on our shoulders we are reminded of how God has blessed us on this earth. And we extol our Lord.

THE LORD'S OWN WAY
Adelaide Addison Pollard

Have thine own way, Lord! Have thine own way!
Thou art the potter, I am the clay.
Mold me and make me after thy will,

While I am waiting, yielded and still.
Have thine own way, Lord! Have thine own way!
Search me and try me, Savior today!
Wash me just now, Lord, wash me just now,
as in thy presence I humbly bow.
Have thine own way, Lord! Have thine own way!
Wounded and weary, help me I pray!
Power, all power, surely is thine!
Touch me and heal me, Savior divine!
Have thine own way, Lord! Have thine own way!
Hold o'er my being absolute sway.
Fill with thy Spirit till all shall see
Christ only, always, living in me!

THE HAND OF GOD

THE POWER of surrendering to God's will for our lives is evident in this hymn by Adelaide A. Pollard, written in 1907. Pollard was struggling with her desire to become a missionary in Africa, but her attempts to raise the necessary funds proved unsuccessful. She attended a prayer meeting and heard another woman surrendering her life to God. Encouraged, Pollard went home and wrote this prayer.

"Have thine own way, Lord!" Pollard understands that we should live not by our will, but by God's will, for God knows best what we need. Often, we struggle on a path we think is right for us only to have our lives take a mysterious detour that leads us into new opportunities and experiences. Is it the hand of God pushing us onto a side road we had never considered?

If we are struggling with a sense of frustration, it is because we have tried to take control rather than listen to the guidance of our inner voice and let life unfold naturally. By trying to force life in a certain direction, usually based upon past illusions, we miss out on the life of purpose and fulfillment God intended for us.

When we allow ourselves to be like clay in the potter's hands, we find we are molded into something far greater than we had envisioned. When we allow our great God to guide our paths, we discover a beautiful life we never imagined possible in our limited thinking. By surrendering to the divine flow of God's love expressed through us, we will experience blessings in abundance. Life will no longer be a struggle; we will no longer be stuck in a rut of our own making.

"Mold me and make me after thy will," Pollard asked willingly in her hymn of faithful surrender all those years ago, and God did answer her, for she not only went on to Africa and Scotland as a missionary but also became a teacher and author of more than 100 hymns and Gospel songs.

What miracles can surrendering to God's loving will bring to your life?

HOW GREAT THOU ART
Carl Boberg

O Lord my God! When I in awesome wonder
Consider all the worlds Thy hands have made.
I see the stars, I hear the rolling thunder,
Thy power through-out the universe displayed.
Then sings my soul, my Savior God, to Thee;
How great Thou art, how great Thou art!
Then sings my soul, my Savior God, to Thee;
How great Thou art, how great Thou art!

FIND GOD IN THE DETAILS

NO ONE CAN DENY the power of nature to inspire awe. That is what happened to Pastor Carl Boberg when he wrote these words of praise in 1886 while watching a raging thunderstorm soon give way to glorious, sunny skies. So strong was the experience of nature's power that Boberg dropped to his knees in adoration of God. He then wrote a nine-stanza poem, which was put to the music of an old Swedish folk melody many years later.

Reading the hymn, we feel Boberg's passionate reminder that God is to be found in the details. If we do not slow down long enough to pay attention to a lovely summer day or a starry night sky, we not only miss the details but also the presence of our Creator, who permeates the universe. As Boberg tells us, God is not just in our churches but also in a roar of thunder, a flash of lightning, or a ray of golden sun breaking through a blanket of thick, gray clouds.

Nature makes the soul sing.

CHAPTER SIX

PRAYERS
of
QUESTIONING

GIVE AND TAKE
Job 1:21

Naked I came from my mother's womb, and naked shall I return there; the Lord gave, and the Lord has taken away; blessed be the name of the Lord.

GOD IS IN CONTROL

JOB WAS living the good life—vast wealth, a loving family, a good reputation, and a commitment to God. This man had it all. Many of the rich people in Scripture are seen as wicked, self-centered, and ignorant of the matters of the soul. Not Job. We're told he was "blameless and upright" (Job 1:1). His seven sons and three daughters would take turns throwing parties, and after each one, he would perform sacrifices on their behalf, just in case there had been any sins committed at those gatherings.

Then the roof fell in—literally. Not only did marauding enemies carry off his herds and kill his servants, but a storm knocked the roof off the house where Job's children were feasting. They were all killed.

Suddenly this rich man was poor. He had nothing left. No flocks. No home. No family—nothing except a complaining wife. And, since everyone assumed that Job must have sinned greatly to cause God to unleash such calamity, he didn't have much of a reputation left either. How did Job respond to such tragedy? He tore his robes and shaved his head—both ancient eastern ways of showing grief—and then he "fell on the ground and worshiped" (Job 1:20). The Hebrew word for worship can refer to a respectful bow before any superior, but it often means falling prostrate before God. In this case Job, mourning deeply, opened his heart to God and prayed this famous prayer.

In 29 words (15 in Hebrew), he set forth a basic philosophy of suffering. Yes, God may rob us of the pleasures we have come to enjoy, but didn't he give them to us originally? How can we blame him for suffering unless we also credit him with joy? He doesn't owe us anything.

Job's wife couldn't understand. As the woes of Job continued and he developed sores all over his body, she said to him, "Are you still holding on to your integrity? Curse God and die" (Job 2:9)! Job's response: "Should we accept only good things from the hand of God and never anything bad?"

Three friends then came to counsel Job. They were sure that Job had sinned greatly, bringing these troubles upon himself. Then another friend, Elihu, arrived and said, "We cannot imagine the power of the Almighty, yet he is so just and merciful that he does not oppress us. No wonder people everywhere fear him. People who are truly wise show him reverence." God himself later confirmed this.

And that point is pretty close to Job's original prayer: "...the Lord gave and the Lord has taken away; blessed be the name of the Lord."

THE ZERO-SUM GAME

IN THE MUSICAL *MY FAIR LADY*, Professor Henry Higgins bets a friend that he can take a common flower girl from the street and make her a proper lady. He selects Eliza Doolittle and gives her a new wardrobe as well as lessons in speaking proper English. After a successful visit to the racetrack with his upper-crust friends, the professor tells Eliza that the bet has been won, the experiment is over, and she should go home.

This is a jolt to Eliza. She has grown accustomed to her life in the professor's home, attended by servants, wearing the finest gowns and jewels. Now she must leave all that behind. As she scolds him for being so callous, he wonders what the problem is. When he took her under his wing, she had nothing. Shouldn't she be grateful for what he had given her? Wasn't it his right to end the experiment?

Technically, he's correct. And that's the point that Job accepts in his prayer. He began life with nothing, and he'll end it in the same way. Whatever he owns he has received from God. God has every right to take it away. In fact, the book of Job lets us know that the calamities that came upon Job were the result of a wager between God and the devil. Would Job remain faithful to God even when everything was taken away? God, like Higgins, was conducting a human experiment.

But there's a greater issue involved, beyond Job's suffering. *My Fair Lady* shows that the professor and the girl become fond of each other. Higgins has a right to end the experiment, but Eliza wants a relationship. The same issue underlies the story of Job. Had the book tried to explain why people suffer, it would have done a pretty poor job of it. But it's not about that. It's about Job's relationship with God. Bad things happen, and Job is faithful. His wife wants him to forget about God, but he will not. His friends belittle him, but he insists, "I know that my Redeemer lives" (Job 19:25). He trusts God through the calamity. Almost as an afterthought, God restores all that Job lost. It was never about his riches. It was Job's faith that won the wager. He continued to bless the name of the Lord.

Bad things have happened to you, no doubt. And, just as Job's friends did, you've tried to figure out why. A loving God would treat you better, wouldn't he? There's plenty of deep thinking you can do on that subject, but don't miss the simple wisdom of Job's prayer. God gives and God takes, but there is always a method in it, though sometimes it is beyond our grasp. These are the times when we must praise God for who he is and trust that he is doing what is best for us.

WHO IS GOD?
Micah 7:18–19

Who is a God like you, pardoning iniquity and passing over the transgression of the remnant of your possession? He does not retain his anger forever, because he delights in showing clemency. He will again have compassion upon us; he will tread our iniquities under foot. You will cast all our sins into the depths of the sea.

A GREAT CHANGE

THE HEBREW PROPHET MICAH asked a question that is good to ask at the beginning of any prayer. The answer is one that has occupied the prayers of many of God's people for centuries.

The Lord is a God who loves us, cares for us, waits for us, and forgives us; he is a God willing to cast all our sins into the sea.

Thinking about who God is—instead of thinking about what we want—changes our prayers. And ultimately it changes us.

HELP FROM THE LORD
Psalm 121:1–3,8

I lift up my eyes to the hills—from where will my help come? My help comes from the Lord, who made heaven and earth.

He will not let your foot be moved; he who keeps you will not slumber....

The Lord will keep your going out and your coming in from this time on and forevermore.

GOD'S PROMISED MERCY

EACH YEAR, the children of Israel ascended the mountains toward Jerusalem for the Holy Days. As they climbed the narrow, rocky trails, they would recite this prayer together.

They looked around them at the many idols in the altars in the high places along the road, and they reminded themselves that their own help came from the Lord, who made the mountains in the first place.

Then they asked the Lord to keep them from falling off the steep and winding trail. They also asked the Lord to protect them from the fierce bandits who hid beside the trail in the dark shadows of the night.

It was a practical prayer about a practical problem. Fortunately, they were praying to a practical God, who promised to show them mercy and who did. Likewise, God's promised mercy is upon us when we place our faith in Christ.

GLIMPSES OF GOD
Francois Chagneau

On what horizon beyond the sea,
In what recess of the earth
is your name inscribed?
In what unknown being
Shall I find you on my way—
You whom I glimpse perhaps
In the motion of a thought
and the uplift of my spirit?
You I have never seen,
Yet in you I believe and hope.

INFINITE LOVE

THE FRENCH COUNTRYSIDE is filled with nearly a hundred abbeys and monasteries, many of them built of stones that have endured for centuries. In the heart of the forest of Boquen stands one of the most simple yet beautiful of these buildings. It is considered a "high place of meditation," whose history goes back to A.D. 1137, when Cistercian monks established it. They remained there until the French Revolution, when the abbey was plundered and fell into disrepair.

In 1936, the antique abbey was rebuilt, stone by stone, rising out of its ruins not only as a building but once again as a center of monastic life that remains vibrant to this day. It currently shelters the Sisters of Bethlehem who, in keeping with their vows of solitude, devote their lives to serving God and humankind.

One of the lay members of the Boquen Abbey, Francois Chagneau, wrote the lines that form a portion of the larger prayer entitled: "Who Are You, My God?" He continues to write prayers for the community at Boquen, prayers that are known for their depth of honesty and sense of longing for a closer walk with God. Here Francois asks the question that fills every heart seeking greater understanding: *Who, exactly, are You? And where can You truly be found?*

It is a quality of the spiritual journey that we, who are finite, can attain only glimpses of the infinite shining through in our everyday experiences. This is the glory of our God, that being Spirit, he is nevertheless revealed to us in the ordinary things of life. Francois speaks of the horizon, the earth, the sea, and even his own thoughts as conveyors of the reality and presence of God.

Are these enough to keep us believing? Though we cannot see the wind, we see its effects. Though we cannot fully "explain" the sunlight, we are warmed by its presence. Although God remains invisible, yet we believe and hope in him; we have experienced him, especially in our most trying moments.

What can be a better blessing from God than knowing God himself? To finally arrive at a firm belief in this unseen Reality, which is infinite Love, is to have our lives changed forever.

PERSISTENT PRAYER
Judges 6:36–40

Then Gideon said to God, "In order to see whether you will deliver Israel by my hand, as you have said, I am going to

lay a fleece of wool on the threshing floor; if there is dew
on the fleece alone, and it is dry on all the ground, then I
shall know that you will deliver Israel by my hand, as you
have said." And it was so. When he rose early next morn-
ing and squeezed the fleece, he wrung enough dew from the
fleece to fill a bowl with water. Then Gideon said to God,
"Do not let your anger burn against me, let me speak one
more time; let me, please, make trial with the fleece just
once more; let it be dry only on the fleece, and on all the
ground let there be dew." And God did so that night. It was
dry on the fleece only, and on all the ground there was dew.

REVERENCE AND FEAR

THIS IS a prayer strategy that should come with a stern warning: "Don't try this at home." Many people have tested God with such prayers, and most have not had Gideon's success. In fact, Moses specifically told the children of Israel, "Do not put the Lord thy God to the test." The context was their demand for God to give them the thing they wanted—the pleasures of Egypt in the Sinai desert.

It's tempting to assume that God should make things easy for us. Gideon's prayer was desperate, however, not presumptuous. It was not about something he wanted, but about something he didn't want—the responsibility of leading his people.

The tribes of Israel were under siege, and when the angel of the Lord appeared to him and called him a "mighty warrior," it was almost laughable. Gideon was a small man, threshing wheat in an ancient winepress so the Midianites wouldn't steal it from him.

If ever anyone needed a sign, Gideon was the man. And that's what he asked for. God was asking him to lead a frightened nation against a frightening army, and Gideon wanted to know for sure that God was truly doing the asking.

Most of the time when we test God, we are looking for help or direction. Gideon was looking for assurance. It was a great task to which he was called, and he needed to know the great God was at his side.

He had the right attitude when he made this request—that is, asking with reverence and fear. He did have the courage to be honest with God, and it changed his life. This timid, reluctant farmer became a leader, a soldier, and a judge. And while he was not presumptuous, he was persistent.

Centuries later, Jesus praised the widow who kept pestering the judge until he did the right thing. This parable, Luke tells us, was intended to "teach us to pray and not give up."

In the face of great adversity, Gideon knew what to do: to be bold before God, and to be willing to ask again.

HERE AM I,
SEND SOMEONE ELSE
Exodus 4:13

O my Lord, please send someone else.

ALLOWING GOD TO USE US

ONE OF the great things about the Bible is its honesty. You might expect a religious book to say only good things about the religious people it portrays. But the Bible shows us the foibles of its main characters. Noah, Abraham and Sarah, Moses, David, Solomon, Elijah—none of these portrayals is spotless. They are shown as real people, with the same doubts, fears, and passions as everyone else.

Moses was possibly the most esteemed figure in Israelite history. After all, he stood up to the mighty Pharaoh of Egypt, demanding "Let my people go!" But how he got to that point—well, the details are less than heroic.

The Israelites worked as slaves in Egypt. Fearing a population boom among these workers, the Egyptians began killing all boys born to the Israelites. Moses' mother saved her son by placing him in a basket of bulrushes and floating him down a river.

Moses was found by Pharaoh's daughter. She adopted little Moses as her own. Moses was reared in Pharaoh's court and accorded the finest education available. But one day a grown-up Moses saw a taskmaster abusing an Israelite slave. After killing the taskmaster, Moses fled into the desert, a fugitive from justice.

In the Sinai desert he made a decent living as a nomadic shepherd, but then an odd sight grabbed his attention. A bush was burning but was not being consumed by the flames. Moses approached it and heard the voice of God.

The Lord said he knew about his people's suffering in Egypt. He wanted to set them free and lead them to a new land. He needed Moses to deliver his message to Pharaoh.

Let's step back a moment and consider the whole breadth of Scripture. God often asks people to do things, and we often hear them responding in faith and obedience. God asks Noah to build an ark, and he does. Young Samuel responds to God's voice with "Speak, for your servant is listening" (1 Samuel 3:10). Isaiah has a vision of God in the temple asking "Whom shall I send" (Isaiah 6:8)? The prophet responds, "Here am I; send me!"

That's not exactly what we get from Moses.

First he stammers, "Who am I?" He's nobody special, and yet God is asking him to do a great thing. God replies that it doesn't matter: "I will be with you."

Moses worries that the Israelites won't even believe God sent him, so God gives him his own name as a calling card—I AM WHO I AM.

Moses isn't buying it: "What if they still don't believe me?" he asks. God gives him miraculous tricks to perform: turning his staff into a snake, making his hand white with leprosy, changing water to blood.

But there's another protest from Moses. "O my Lord, I have never been eloquent,...I am slow of speech and slow of tongue." God points out that he created Moses' tongue. "I will...teach you what you are to speak."

All out of excuses, Moses cries out his prayer: "Please send someone else!" Finally the Lord gets upset with Moses, but he agrees to send Moses' brother, Aaron, as a spokesman.

SECRET SERVICE

WE'RE BEING a bit tough on Moses here, but only because we've all been there. We live our lives in comfort zones, but sometimes we get a sense that God wants us to try something new. Perhaps you might teach a fifth-grade Sunday school class, invite a neighbor to your small-group

Bible study, or make friends with the coworker who just moved here from another state or country.

And we tend to trot out all of Moses' excuses. Who am I, Lord? I don't have the talents required. I love you, Lord, but don't ask me to do that. Send someone else.

If you've prayed this prayer of Moses lately, don't feel guilty. You're in good company. But understand that when you run out of excuses the voice will still be calling. If you let God lead you on a new adventure, you might be surprised at what he can do through you.

Amazingly, God used Moses to do mighty things in spite of all his excuses. He confronted the Pharaoh, supported by his brother Aaron, and he led his people out of slavery. He became the nation's greatest leader but not because he wanted to be. He simply allowed the Lord to push him out of his comfort zone. Let God do the same for you.

THE SINGING FIRE
Psalm 77:4–9

You keep my eyelids from closing; I am so troubled that I cannot speak. I consider the days of old, and remember the years of long ago. I commune with my heart in the night; I meditate and search my spirit: "Will the Lord spurn forever, and never again be favorable? Has his steadfast love ceased forever? Are his promises at an end for all time? Has God forgotten to be gracious? Has he in anger shut up his compassion?"

GOD'S REVELATION

SUSANNAH SPURGEON, wife of the famous English preacher, was bedridden for 15 years. One night, after a particularly long and restless day, she says the darkness entered her very soul, and she prayed, asking God, "Why do you permit lingering weakness to hinder the sweet service I long to render to your poor servants?"

There was no answer, and the only sound she heard was the crackling of an oak log in the fireplace. Suddenly, however, she heard a clear musical note, like the trill of a robin and wondered where it was coming from, considering both the time of year and the time of day.

Eventually she realized what it was. In her words, "The fire was letting loose the imprisoned music from the old oak's innermost heart!" This event deeply moved her. Later, she wrote that "when the fire of affliction draws songs of praise from us, then indeed we are purified, and our God is glorified."

Like the psalmist, she spent countless restless nights praying and weeping and searching. And like the psalmist she at last found both strength and joy in God's beautiful revelation of himself, which often comes only in our darkest, loneliest hours.

St. John of the Cross, while imprisoned for his faith, called this the "dark night of the soul," and he said it was not only likely but also necessary if we are to grow deeper in our spiritual life.

Only then, like Susannah, will we hear singing in the fire.

COMFORT FOODS
Psalm 42:1–5

As a deer longs for flowing streams, so my soul longs for you, O God. My soul thirsts for God, for the living God. When shall I come and behold the face of God? My tears have been my food day and night, while people say to me continually, "Where is your God?"

These things I remember, as I pour out my soul: how I went with the throng, and led them in procession to the house of God, with glad shouts and songs of thanksgiving, a multitude keeping festival. Why are you cast down, O my soul, and why are you disquieted within me? Hope in God; for I shall again praise him, my help and my God.

OUR NEED FOR GOD

THINK OF a delicious food or drink you love, not because you need it, but because the mere taste of it brings you great joy. All of us have such foods. We call them comfort foods, foods that remind us of home and make us feel secure.

Often our comfort foods and drinks are not fancy or expensive. They just evoke powerful memories and relationships, creating a thirst or appetite for the familiar and for the sacred.

For each of us, there is some great longing for which there are few satisfactions. In the same way a deer bounding through the forest pants for a drink from a cool, fresh spring, we all long for something satisfying, and in this prayer we are reminded that this longing is a picture of our soul's own great need for God.

This longing is palatable and insatiable. The closer we get to God, the thirstier for him we become. According to St. Bernard of Clairvaux, we first taste the sweetness of God in our prayers, and then "Once the sweetness of God has been tasted, it draws us to the pure love of God more than our needs compel us to love him." In other words, we eventually want God's love more than anything else God could give us. In one of his hymns, Bernard wrote:

> We taste Thee, O Thou Living Bread,
> And long to feast upon Thee still:
> We drink of Thee, the Fountainhead
> And thirst our souls from Thee to fill.

It is this craving that leads the psalmist to "the house of God, with glad shouts and songs of thanksgiving." And it is this craving that prayer creates as it changes our deepest desire.

A BARGAIN WITH GOD
Micah 6:6–8

"With what shall I come before the Lord, and bow myself before God on high? Shall I come before him with burnt offerings, with calves a year old? Will the Lord be pleased with thousands of rams, with ten thousands of rivers of oil? Shall I give my firstborn for my transgression, the fruit of my body for the sin of my soul?" He has told you, O mortal, what is good; and what does the Lord require of you but to do justice, and to love kindness, and to walk humbly with your God?

LOVE GOD

MICAH OF MORESHETH tells us that God requires only that we be just, kind, and humble. Yet, how often do we think that we must offer "bargaining chips" in order to get our prayers answered and make God smile down upon us? How often do we barter with God to get what we want when all God wants is for us to walk in his ways?

What God requires is not burnt offerings—calves, rams, or rivers of oil. God cares not for material goods. After all, he made them! What God requires of us is simply what Jesus taught his disciples: Love God with all your heart, soul, and mind, and love your neighbor as yourself. That's all it takes.

CHAPTER SEVEN

PRAYERS
of
REPENTANCE
and
RECOMMITMENT

CONFESSIONS AND FORGIVENESS
Psalm 38:1-4, 9-11, 17-22

❧❧❧

O Lord, do not rebuke me in your anger, or discipline me in your wrath. For your arrows have sunk into me, and your hand has come down on me.

There is no soundness in my flesh because of your indignation; there is no health in my bones because of my sin. For my iniquities have gone over my head; they weigh like a burden too heavy for me...

O Lord, all my longing is known to you; my sighing is not hidden from you. My heart throbs, my strength fails me; as for the light of my eyes—it also has gone from me. My friends and companions stand aloof from my affliction, and my neighbors stand far off...

I am ready to fall, and my pain is ever with me. I confess my iniquity; I am sorry for my sin. Those who are my foes without cause are mighty, and many are those who hate me wrongfully. Those who render me evil for good are my adversaries because I follow after good.

Do not forsake me, O Lord; O my God, do not be far from me; make haste to help me, O Lord, my salvation.

ACKNOWLEDGING OUR WEAKNESSES

FOR MANY PEOPLE, the path to God begins with a sincere confession—acknowledging our failures while throwing ourselves at the mercy of our God. It is a habit that has fallen out of fashion. In our world, guilt is considered a bad thing, and blame always belongs to someone else.

Yet, that is not the world where the saints lived. Each of them at some point fell down before God, and they always found mercy. This was the experience of David, who confessed his weakness in this psalm and cried for God to save him.

Jesus tells us to ask God to forgive our sins. This shouldn't be too hard; as this prayer says, our longing is known to him. Naming our sins and turning from them is the first step toward God. The next steps are humility and strength.

Before God we find forgiveness and freedom. Confession seems like a small price to pay.

JONAH'S PRAYER
Jonah 2:1–9

Then Jonah prayed to the Lord his God from the belly of the fish, saying, "I called to the Lord out of my distress, and he answered me; out of the belly of Sheol I cried, and you heard my voice. You cast me into the deep, into the heart of the seas, and the flood surrounded me; all your waves and your billows passed over me. Then I said, 'I am driven away from your sight; how shall I look again upon your holy temple?' The waters closed in over me; the deep surrounded me; weeds were wrapped around my head at the roots of the mountains. I went down to the land whose bars closed upon me forever; yet you brought up my life from the Pit, O Lord my God. As my life was ebbing away, I remembered the Lord; and my prayer came to you, into your holy temple. Those who worship vain idols forsake their true loyalty. But I with the voice of thanksgiving will sacrifice to you; what I have vowed I will pay. Deliverance belongs to the Lord!

NEVER HIDE FROM GOD

THE STORY OF JONAH in the belly of a great fish is a powerful example of what happens to our lives when we do not obey the will of God. Often we are blessed with intuitive guidance—the whisper of God directing our path. Yet, sometimes we second-guess the wisdom God has taught us and pay the price for it, as Jonah did.

The Lord told Jonah he wanted him to go to Nineveh to protest the wickedness of the people there. Instead of obeying God, Jonah ran away. He hid on board a ship, but when a storm nearly sank the ship, the crew cast him overboard as a sacrifice to the Lord. Jonah paid the price for disregarding the Lord's command by nearly drowning in the raging sea.

In his mercy, however, the Lord gave Jonah an intriguing second chance by having a large fish swallow him whole. This fish ironically gave Jonah shelter for three days and nights. During this time, Jonah sorrowfully realized how badly he had disobeyed God, and he prayed this prayer of praise.

Jonah cried out from the belly of this fish, praising God for not letting him drown and for bringing his life "up from the Pit." We often act like Jonah when we realize we have not followed the Lord's divine guidance. We get lost from the path that God set before us, and we cry out to God to help us find our way back.

Not only did God answer Jonah's cries of distress, but God also spoke to the fish, and it spewed Jonah out onto dry land. Again, God requested that Jonah go to Nineveh. This time, Jonah obeyed.

If you believe in your heart there is something God wants you to do—that God is telling you to do something—do not disobey God. If you do, you will pay experience being cast out into the open sea of guilt and despair. Learn from Jonah: If we follow God's will the first time around, our lives will be a lot easier in the long run.

FORGIVE ME, LORD
Act of Contrition

My God, I am sorry for my sins with all my heart. In choosing to do wrong and failing to do good, I have sinned against you whom I should love above all things. I firmly intend, with your help, to do penance, to sin no more, and to avoid whatever leads me to sin.

TAKE RESPONSIBILITY

MILLIONS OF PEOPLE have spoken this prayer as part of their confession, asking God to forgive them for their sins and offenses. As we grow in our faith in Christ, we continue to fall short of the mark. Therefore, we repeat this reverent prayer to God, offering repentance and pleading for grace.

We detest it when we sin, but because we have human weaknesses, we fail now and then. Therefore, we must look to God for the promise of heaven that awaits those who come before him and ask for forgiveness. This requires humility, honesty, and the courage to take responsibility for our mistakes.

No matter who we are, we sin. When we do, we know we can go before God to make amends; we can do what is necessary to walk once again in his light. We vow to do better each day as we grow as Christians.

A PRAYER OF CONFESSION
Book of Common Prayer

Most merciful God, we confess that we have sinned against you in thought, word, and deed, by what we have done, and by what we have left undone. We have not loved you with our whole heart; we have not loved our neighbors as ourselves.

We are truly sorry and we humbly repent.

For the sake of your Son Jesus Christ, have mercy on us and forgive us; that we may delight in your will, and walk in your ways, to the glory of your Name. Amen.

NEVER DESPAIR

A WRITER ONCE SPOKE of a distressing experience of loss. He had left his only copy of four chapters of a new book in a hotel room drawer. When he called to retrieve that priceless stack of papers, the manager told him they'd been thrown away. The man was devastated. He thought of the months of energy that had gone into polishing those four chapters. He imagined trying to start over, trying to recover just the right words again, knowing it would be impossible. But then—salvation! Two weeks later a cleaning woman called to say she had found the papers. All was not lost, after all.

The story of a lost manuscript reminds us that our spiritual salvation is first and foremost about being unfaithful, about sinning, about being truly lost to begin with. Yes, that awareness must come first. Sometimes we forget our condition, or we attempt to rationalize our sins. Unfortunately, if we ignore our true state, we only weaken our understanding of what God's gracious search-and-rescue mission is all about.

At the same time, we must never despair in the face of our inconsistent lives, our crazy addictions, or our repeated failures at living faithfully. God is always looking for people just like us. In fact, when the Pharisees asked Jesus why he ate and drank with tax collectors and sinners, Jesus responded: "It is not the healthy who need a doctor, but the sick. I have not come to call the righteous, but sinners" (Mark 2:17, NIV).

Offering a prayer of confession like this is the first step in changing the entire direction of our lives. Often, when we walk away from a person or situation, the door immediately closes behind us and stays forever sealed tight. When we walk away from God and his will, however, we can always return.

Therefore, let us acknowledge our loss and cry for God's mercy. For only as we utter our confessions can we receive the priceless blessing of God's forgiveness.

A KING'S CONFESSION
Psalm 51:1–17

Have mercy on me, O God, according to your steadfast love; according to your abundant mercy blot out my transgressions. Wash me thoroughly from my iniquity, and cleanse me from my sin.

For I know my transgressions, and my sin is ever before me. Against you, you alone, have I sinned, and done what is evil in your sight, so that you are justified in your sentence and blameless when you pass judgment. Indeed, I was born guilty, a sinner when my mother conceived me.

You desire truth in the inward being; therefore teach me wisdom in my secret heart. Purge me with hyssop, and I shall be clean; wash me, and I shall be whiter than snow.

Let me hear joy and gladness; let the bones that you have crushed rejoice. Hide your face from my sins, and blot out all my iniquities.

Create in me a clean heart, O God, and put a new and right spirit within me. Do not cast me away from your presence, and do not take your holy spirit from me. Restore to me the joy of your salvation, and sustain in me a willing spirit.

Then I will teach transgressors your ways, and sinners will return to you. Deliver me from bloodshed, O God, O God of my salvation, and my tongue will sing aloud of your deliverance.

O Lord, open my lips, and my mouth will declare your praise. For you have no delight in sacrifice; if I were to give a burnt offering, you would not be pleased. The sacrifice acceptable to God is a broken spirit; a broken and contrite heart, O God, you will not despise.

A PSALM OF SORROW FOR SIN

THE KING had committed adultery. In his attempt to hide his sin, he had the woman's husband killed. In most nations, this wouldn't have been a problem. Kings let their lusts run freely. But in Israel, the king didn't call the shots—God did. So when the prophet Nathan confronted King David with his sin, the king knew he had to repent publicly (2 Samuel 11–12).

It had started on a flat rooftop as David strolled there, probably to cool off in the evening. He spied Bathsheba bathing on a rooftop across the way, and he wanted her. The king sent for her and slept with her, and she became pregnant. Since her husband was off fighting in the army, it would be plain to all that the birth was illegitimate. The shame would eventually make its way back to David.

So he attempted a cover-up worthy of modern politics. Calling the husband back from battle, the king rewarded him for his good service, offering him some time with his wife. Then people would think the child-to-be belonged to the husband. A great plan—except the loyal soldier refused to enjoy his wife's company while his fellow soldiers were still in battle. The husband slept outside the king's door. Finally David sent the husband back to the front lines with a secret message for the general: Get into fierce fighting and pull back. In other words: Make sure this man dies.

The plan worked. In a magnanimous gesture, King David married the widow of this war hero and offered to raise the child as his own. What a great monarch! As far as anyone knew, David was a paragon of virtue in this matter. But God knew otherwise, and he sent the prophet Nathan to David with a parable.

There was a situation the king needed to know about, said the prophet. A rich man with many flocks, desiring the only lamb of his poor neighbor, stole that lamb and ate it for dinner. Hearing this, David was livid. How could such injustice occur in his kingdom? "That man deserves to die!" the king raged.

"You are the man," Nathan replied, and David was cut to the quick. God struck the newborn baby with a deadly illness, leading David to begin a very public repentance, fasting and throwing himself on the ground. David begged God to spare the child's life, but the child died within a week.

Some time later, according to the title sentence attached to Psalm 51, David wrote his song of confession. It's an amazing cry of the heart, a plea for forgiveness. It's all the more remarkable because of the public nature of these words. The innermost feelings of Israel's king were being broadcast, printed up in the nation's hymnal. But as a result, this psalm has been used by countless believers as a model for their own repentance.

A NEED FOR CLEANSING

THIS PSALM has many descriptions of forgiveness. Most of them have to do with washing. Elsewhere David prays that his sins be "covered" (Psalm 32:1), but maybe at this time he's had too much covering up. He needs something far more radical—a thorough cleansing inside and out.

Note also that the basis for forgiveness is God's mercy and steadfast love—it's not that David deserves it. God forgives sin because it is in his nature to do so. When we wander from God, he wants us to return to him. So if we look to God for guidance and forgiveness, he will help us.

This is something to remember as we come to God in repentance. Often in our human interactions we ask for forgiveness based on the triviality of the offense ("I didn't mean it") or our own general goodness ("I won't do it again"). Sometimes we even demand forgiveness because of our good track record ("After all I've done for you!"). But none of that is appropriate with God. He has every right to cast us away from his presence. But instead, because of his loving mercy, he cleans, washes, restores, and sustains.

Christian theologians are tantalized by a couple of points in this psalm. It touches on the idea of original sin, though this could also be David's poetic lament over his inability to do right. There is the mention of the "holy spirit" of God—long before the New Testament developed the doctrine of the Trinity. Salvation is another concept more commonly associated with the New Testament that shows up here. David asks God to restore "the joy of [God's] salvation." This warrior had experienced God's deliverance on many occasions. Is he praying for a spiritual deliverance here, or does he long for the joy that comes from knowing God will once again be on his side? Notice that the "joy of salvation" is placed parallel to David's own willing spirit. As we pray this psalm, we might find the same parallel: We're on the same page with God; we eagerly participate in his plans for us.

Toward the end of this psalm, David promises to speak out about God and his ways. The time for secrecy is over. David will offer both praise to God and instruction to other sinners. As a result, many people would "turn to God."

When we do something wrong, God always desires to forgive us and begin anew. Are you truly sorry for your sins? Then pray the prayer of David, and ask for forgiveness from our loving, merciful God.

A SINNER'S PRAYER
Luke 18:13

God, be merciful to me, a sinner!

GOD IS MERCIFUL

TAX COLLECTORS were a hated people in Jesus' day. First, they were traitors, collecting money from their fellow Jews on behalf of the despised Roman government. Second, they weren't nice about it at all. Tax collectors would charge extra to increase their own profit. If someone argued, the collectors could call in some thugs from the Roman army for some additional "persuasion." Tax collectors would take things from people's houses and beat those who could not pay—all with the protection of Rome. Because of their collaboration with the Romans, tax collectors were naturally shunned from the religious life of Israel. Because of their entanglements with "unclean" Gentiles, tax collectors had no chance of following Jewish law.

In the gospels, we often find tax collectors lumped together with prostitutes. Together, these groups were the lowest of the low, rejected by society. As most people saw it, these sinners had given up any hope of a relationship with God.

On the other hand, the Pharisees were a respected people in Jesus' day. They devoted their lives to keeping God's law. Pharisees sought God's favor as an eager student seeks a teacher's approval. They were the first to answer the tough religious questions, and they were always sure to let everyone know how well they knew God.

Officially, their hope was to usher in the Messiah's arrival by making the nation righteous. To do this, they added extra laws to God's laws. They wanted to "build a hedge" around the scriptural commands so that people wouldn't even come close to breaking them.

HUMBLE HEARTS ARE HEARD IN HEAVEN

BUT JESUS HAD a way of turning everything around. He told a simple story of two people going to the temple to pray—a Pharisee and a tax collector. Jesus' listeners would wonder what a tax collector was doing anywhere close to the temple. The Pharisee belonged there, but the tax collector didn't.

In Jesus' story, the Pharisee prays first, boasting about his religious achievements. He thanks God that he is not as sinful as others—like that tax collector standing nearby.

The tax collector had a completely different attitude. He was "standing far off." The Pharisee had taken center stage while the tax collector tried to melt into the scenery. This humble sinner would not even look up toward heaven, as most people did in prayer; he beat his chest as a sign of despair and uttered this basic prayer.

Try to put yourself in the crowd of Jesus' listeners. Tax collectors have taken your money, but Pharisees seem to be good people. As you hear this tax collector in Jesus' story asking for mercy, your reaction might be: "After all you've done, how dare you ask for mercy!" And then you hear the conclusion of the story. It was the tax collector who went home justified before God, not the Pharisee. Jesus shows us that God exalts the ultimate sinner who is humble while he humbles the proud.

The Pharisees may have meant well, but somewhere along the way their desire for worldly status replaced their desire to serve God. With all the praise they received from others they no longer saw themselves as sinners. Trying to live a good life is commendable. The problem comes when we forget that each of us has faults. The Bible tells us that "all have sinned and fall short of the glory of God" (Romans 3:23). God can work with us only when we recognize this truth.

Maybe you know someone who is "cleanliness-challenged." Such people might want to have a clean room, but they have a hard time seeing the dirt that's there and knowing what "clean" truly looks like. One apartment-dweller might run a rag over a counter and say it's clean, but a roommate comes along and says, "It's still filthy!" It's not a lack of desire; it's a lack of knowing and of practice—of taking the time to reflect and see the difference.

The Pharisees were blind to the dirt in their souls. They needed God's mercy, but they didn't know enough to ask for it. The tax collector recognized his sin and his need for mercy. So should we.

ALL AND NOTHING
St. Francis of Assisi

Let us therefore desire nothing else, wish for nothing else, and let nothing please and delight us except our Creator and Redeemer, and Savior, the only true God, who is full of good, who alone is good,... and from whom, and through whom, and in whom is all mercy, all grace, all glory of all penitents and of the just, and of all the blessed rejoicing in heaven.

LASTING GRACE

For St. Francis, it's all *and* nothing, not all *or* nothing. If we receive only God's gifts, we end up with all the joy heaven offers. When we surrender to the Lord, we get everything that matters. We give up things that don't last, and we receive things that do. It's not a bad trade.

PRAYER AND ACTION
St. Thomas More

The things, good Lord, that we pray for, give us the grace to labour for.

FAITH MOTIVATES

We can easily ask that God's will be done without wanting it to require any work from us. Yet, God finds ways to arouse our interest until we become thoroughly involved. Our prayers mean the most when we're demonstrating their importance by our actions.

Most would agree with the apostle James that faith without corresponding actions has little value. Have you found it to be true in your own life? What is motivating you to help your neighbor at this moment? Ideally, you have already prayed for him or her and are now ready to reach out a loving, helping hand!

SURRENDERING OUR HEARTS
Book of Common Prayer

Almighty God,
unto whom all hearts be open,
all desires known,
and from whom no secrets are hid:
Cleanse the thoughts of our hearts,
by the inspiration of thy Holy Spirit:
that we may perfectly love thee,
and worthily magnify thy holy name.

FOCUS ON THE INSIDE

THE TRULY LIFE-CHANGING PRAYER of complete surrender is to ask God not only to cleanse us from our sinful deeds but also to purge the sinful thoughts of our hearts. For what we are doing on the outside is surely no larger a concern to God than what we are quickly becoming on the inside.

When we surrender ourselves to God this way, he will transform our character. Then the world will see the Lord living in us despite the failures in our lives.

EARNEST ENTREATIES
From the Roman Missal

Grant, we beseech Thee, Almighty God, that we may so please Thy Holy Spirit by our earnest entreaties, that we may by His grace both be freed from all temptations and merit to receive the forgiveness of our sins. Through Christ our Lord, Amen.

THE HEALING POWER OF FORGIVENESS

THERE IS NOTHING so empowering as God's grace; it brings us freedom from evil and forgiveness for our past sins. In prayer, we offer up our "earnest entreaties," appealing for God's mercy and knowing God will answer our request.

The power of forgiveness lies in its ability to free us from the weight of past resentments, anger, and conflict. It makes us feel lighter and more open to life. Forgiveness heals, and that healing begins when we first go to God for redemption and renewal.

SPREADING THE WORD
John 11:41–42

Father, I thank you for having heard me. I knew that you always hear me, but I have said this for the sake of the crowd standing here, so that they may believe that you sent me.

SHOW WHAT GOD'S LOVE CAN DO

JESUS WANTED the crowd to understand that God had sent him. That's why he publicly raised Lazarus from the dead, performing a miracle with God's mighty power working through him. When we witness the wonderful works of our heavenly Father, it is only natural to want to show those wonders to others. In Jesus' case, he was validating his unique role as the Savior of humankind.

As Christians, we walk a fine line between wanting to share our love of God with others and not wanting to overwhelm them with our spirituality. Being a good witness means letting our joy-filled lives stand as the best proof of what God's love can do. Just as Jesus did when he raised Lazarus from the dead, it is best to show, not tell.

When we walk in the light and let God work through us, we attract others to us, for they will want to know what motivates us. Then we will best be able to share the good news about Jesus the Savior.